"双高计划"双语教学教材

Specialized English for Chemistry and Chemical Engineering

化学化工专业英语

程 进 樊亚娟 主编

·北京·

内容简介

《化学化工专业英语》依据最新的国家及行业标准，通过分析主要职业岗位工作任务和课程内容，确定了本教材的大纲和主体内容。

本教材涵盖科技基础英语、化学化工专业英语和实践英语3部分：在整体编排上既涵盖科技基础英语、科技文献等通用内容，也涵盖"五大化学""三传一反"等化学化工专业核心技术内容；既选用了化学化工领域的典型与前沿内容文章，也在提炼列举了常用的短语短句；既通过词汇、句型讲解提升学生读写的能力，也通过场景会话的训练提升学生听说的能力；既提供了传统的图片、音频等静态资源，也提供"AI搜一搜"栏目的关键词，引导学生利用AI生成动态资源。

本书可作为化工技术类相关专业的高等职业教育教材，也可供相关行业的科研及生产一线技术人员阅读参考，同时也可作为企业职工培训资料。

图书在版编目（CIP）数据

化学化工专业英语 / 程进，樊亚娟主编. -- 北京：化学工业出版社，2024.9. --（"双高计划"双语教学教材）. -- ISBN 978-7-122-46283-1

I. H31

中国国家版本馆CIP数据核字第20241JZ888号

责任编辑：吕　尤　徐雅妮
责任校对：王　静　　　　　　　　装帧设计：韩　飞

出版发行：化学工业出版社
　　　　（北京市东城区青年湖南街13号　邮政编码100011）
印　　刷：三河市航远印刷有限公司
装　　订：三河市宇新装订厂
787mm×1092mm　1/16　印张 8¾　字数176千字
2024年11月北京第1版第1次印刷

购书咨询：010-64518888　　　　　　售后服务：010-64518899
网　　址：http://www.cip.com.cn

凡购买本书，如有缺损质量问题，本社销售中心负责调换。

定　　价：38.00元　　　　　　　　　　　　版权所有　违者必究

前　言

当今世界正处于百年未有之大变局，人类文明发展面临越来越多的问题和挑战。中国着眼人类前途命运和整体利益，因应全球发展及各国期待，继承和弘扬丝路精神这一人类文明的宝贵遗产，提出共建"一带一路"倡议。这一倡议为化学化工行业学生更好地融入国际环境提出了更高的要求，具备专业英语能力已成为化学化工领域人才的重要素质。

为对接化工行业这一人才素质培养要求，我们编写了这本《化学化工专业英语》教材，旨在提升学生的专业英语水平，为他们的未来职业生涯奠定坚实的基础。本书内容特色如下：

（1）面向化工实验室开发、化工企业生产以及化学化工相关产品现代服务等岗位需求，设置了科技基础英语、化学化工专业英语和实践英语3部分，共9章，包括：科学英语基础、文献英语、"五大化学"英语（无机化学、有机化学、分析化学、物理化学、高分子化学）、"三传一反"英语（动量传递工程、热量传递工程、质量传递工程、化学反应工程）、实验室实践英语、化工生产现场实践英语。所选范文难易适中，内容新颖，语言规范。

（2）本书在每一章节的开头设置了"AI搜一搜，了解知识背景"栏目，帮助读者快速掌握本章的背景知识；在章节中间加入了"AI搜一搜，获取学习资源"栏目，方便读者获取更多相关的学习资源，拓展知识面；在章节末尾补充了"AI搜一搜，检验学习效果"栏目，帮助读者自我测试，巩固所学内容。

（3）本书不仅包括以专业基础知识为主的课文、常用的专业词汇和常用句型，还包括考查专业英语应用能力的互动训练，及时巩固读者对专业词汇和句型的掌握。

（4）除每节后的互动练习外，每单元还包括"Speak & Listen""Write & Read"单元练习，进一步提升化学化工专业英语的听说读写能力。这些也可以作为课堂教学的互动和测试环节，不仅为课程学习提供了素材和内容支持，也为课堂教学提供了环节支持。

本教材由常州工程职业技术学院程进、樊亚娟主编，乔奇伟、刘健副主编，瑞士罗氏化学（中国）集团的吴俊博士主审。其中第1、8章由乔奇伟编写，第2章由刘健编写，第 3、4、5、7 章及课后互动练习由程进编写，第 6 章由刘长春编写，第 9 章由樊亚娟编写，全书由程进统稿。编写过程中，我们得到了化学工业出版社的大力支持以及巴斯夫原高级经理 Axel Hildebrandt 博士的帮助。同时，我们在高阅读性方面的构思也受到了日本知名作家斋藤胜裕的《化学版 これを英語で言えますか》（化学版）启发。在此，感谢为本教材出版给予帮助的专家和老师。

我们真诚地希望本书能为广大师生的教与学提供有力的支持，同时也期待读者在使用过程中提出宝贵的意见和建议，以便我们不断完善和提高。

编　者

2024 年 3 月

目 录

Part 1　General English for Science and Technology

1 Fundamental Science English　2
1.1 Common Units and Expressions　2
1.2 Numbers and Mathematical Expressions　8
1.3 Graphics and Charts　14
Exercises　19

2 Literature English　22
2.1 Components of General Literature　22
2.2 Main Components and Common Terms of the Body Text　26
2.3 Presentation and Common Terms in Experimental Results　30
Exercises　35

Part 2　Specialized English for Chemistry and Chemical Engineering

3 Basics of Chemistry　38
3.1 Inorganic Chemistry　38
3.2 Organic Chemistry　42
3.3 Analytical Chemistry　45
3.4 Physical Chemistry　49
3.5 Polymer Chemistry　53
Exercises　57

4 Momentum Transfer Process　60
4.1 Fluid Mechanics Principles　60
4.2 Fluid Transport Equipment　64

4.3 Non-Homogeneous Separation Equipment   71

Exercises   76

5 Heat Transfer Process   78
5.1 Principles and Processes of Heat Transfer   78

5.2 Heat Transfer Equipment   82

Exercises   86

6 Mass Transfer Process   88
6.1 Principles of Mass Transfer   88

6.2 Mass Transfer Equipment   92

Exercises   96

7 Chemical Reaction Process   98
7.1 Chemical Reaction Kinetics Principles   98

7.2 Chemical Reaction Processes   102

7.3 Chemical Reaction Equipment   106

Exercises   111

Part 3　Practical English for Chemical Engineering

8 Chemical Laboratory Practical English   114
8.1 Laboratory Apparatus and Operation   114

8.2 Commonly Used Conversation in Chemical Laboratory   119

Exercises   121

9 Chemical Production Practical English   124
9.1 Commonly Used English in Chemical Production   124

9.2 Common Spoken English in Chemical Production   128

Exercises   131

Reference   133

Part 1

General English for Science and Technology

　　毋庸置疑，化学（chemistry）及化学工程（chemical engineering）都是科学的重要分支。因此，有必要在学习化学化工专业英语之初，先学习科学基础英语。

1

Fundamental Science English

朗读二维码

搜一搜，
了解专业背景

....

化学常用单位

化学数字表示

化学图表表示

....

搜一搜，
获取学习资源

....

化学常用单位的视频

化学数字表示的视频

化学图表表示的视频

....

1.1 Common Units and Expressions

In the field of chemistry, quantitative determination and analysis are essential components of experimental procedures. These processes require precise measurements of the amount, quantity, volume, and content of substances involved in chemical reactions. In order to communicate these measurements accurately, a standardized system of units and expressions has been developed.

(1) Unit

A unit is a defined quantity of a particular physical property used as a standard for measurement. As shown in Figure 1-1, the most commonly used units in chemistry are the SI (International System of Units) units, which are based on the metric system.

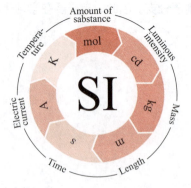

Figure 1-1 Common scientific units of the International System of Units

(2) Avogadro Constant

Avogadro Constant is a fundamental constant used in chemistry to describe the size of a mole. It represents the number of atoms or molecules in one mole of a substance, which is approximately 6.022×10^{23}.

(3) Mole

The mole is a unit of measurement used in chemistry to quantify the amount of a substance. One mole is defined as the amount of substance that contains as many elementary entities (such as atoms or molecules) as there are atoms in 12 grams of carbon-12.

(4) Atomic Weight

The atomic weight is the mass of an atom, usually expressed in atomic mass units (amu). As Figure 1-2 depicted, it is calculated as the sum of the number of protons and neutrons in the nucleus of an atom.

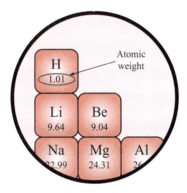

Figure 1-2　A corner of the periodic table of elements

(5) Molecular Weight

Molecular weight is the sum of the atomic weights of all the atoms in a molecule. It is expressed in atomic mass units (amu) or in grams per mole (g/mol).

(6) Concentration

Concentration is the amount of a substance per unit volume of a solution. It is expressed in various units such as molar concentration (mol/L), mole fraction, percent concentration of mass or weight, parts per thousand (ppt), parts per million (ppm), or parts per billion (ppb).

(7) Molarity

Molarity is a unit of concentration that expresses the number of moles of solute per liter of solution (mol/L).

(8) Solution

As shown in Figure 1-3, a solution is a homogeneous mixture of two or more substances, the substance present in the larger amount is called the solvent, the substance present in the smaller amount is called the solute, and the process of adding the solute into the solvent is called solvation.

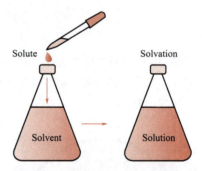

Figure 1-3 Solution composition

(9) Temperature

Temperature is a measure of the average kinetic energy of the particles in a substance. As shown in Figure 1-4, it is usually measured in degrees of Celsius (°C), Fahrenheit (°F) or Kelvin (K).

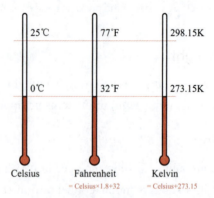

Figure 1-4 Comparison of three temperature modes

(10) Pressure

Pressure is the force exerted per unit area. It is usually measured in pascal (Pa) or atmospheres (atm). Figure 1-5 showed the commonly used U-type pressure gauge in pressure measurement.

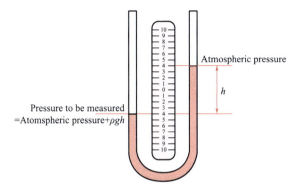

Figure 1-5　U-type pressure gauge

（11）Volume

Volume is the amount of space occupied by a substance. It is usually measured in liters (L), milliliters (mL), or microliters (μL).

（12）Weight

Weight is the force exerted on a body due to the acceleration of gravity. It is usually measured in grams (g), kilograms (kg), or milligrams (mg).

Conclusion

In conclusion, the use of standardized units and expressions is crucial in communicating quantitative measurements in the field of chemistry. It is important to be familiar with these units and expressions in order to accurately perform and interpret chemical experiments.

专业词汇

- quantitative determination　定量测定
- quantitative analysis　定量分析
- quantification　定量化
- mount, quantity　数量

朗读二维码

- volume   体积
- content   含量
- unit   单位
- Avogadro's number   阿伏伽德罗数
- atom   原子
- molecular   分子的
- ion   离子
- mole   摩尔
- atomic mass   原子质量
- absolute number   绝对数
- weight   重量
- numeric value   数值
- molecular weight   分子量
- concentration   浓度
- molar(mol) concentration   摩尔浓度
- molarity   摩尔浓度
- liter   升
- solution   溶液
- solute   溶质
- amount of substance   物质的量
- substance quantity   物质的量
- mole per liter   摩尔/升
- molar fraction   摩尔分数
- solvent   溶剂
- percent concentration of mass   质量分数
- weight percentage   质量分数
- percent   百分比
- parts per thousand   千分之
- ppm   百万分之
- ppb   十亿分之
- state   状态
- situation   情况
- condition   条件
- temperature   温度
- room temperature   室温
- Celsius degree   摄氏度
- Fahrenheit degree   华氏度
- pressure   压力
- atmospheric pressure   大气压力

- ordinary pressure   标准大气压力
- reduced pressure   减压
- increasing pressure   增压
- milliliter (mL)   毫升
- microliter   微升
- mass   质量
- gram   克
- kilogram   千克
- milligram   毫克

常用句型

- **The most commonly used** units in chemistry are the SI (International System of Units) units, which are based on the metric system. 化学中最常用的单位是基于公制的 SI 单位制 (国际单位制)。

【句型解释】这个句型采用了 "**the most ... are**" 的结构，表示 "最多的 ..." 或 "最常见的 ..."，同时用了 "**commonly used**" 来形容单位，强调了它们的普及性和重要性。

【例句】The **most commonly used** measurement unit for length in the scientific community is meters. 在科学界中，长度最常用的测量单位是米。

互动练习

- What is the unit of measurement for volume? (   )
   A) Liter
   B) Gram
   C) Kilogram
   D) Milligram
- What is the unit of measurement for weight? (   )
   A) Liter
   B) Gram
   C) Kilogram
   D) Milligram
- What is the unit of measurement for concentration? (   )
   A) Liter

B) Gram

C) Molarity

D) Mol per liter

- What is the unit of measurement for pressure? (　　)

  A) Liter

  B) Gram

  C) Kilogram

  D) Pascal

- What is the unit of measurement for temperature on the Celsius scale? (　　)

  A) Kelvin

  B) Fahrenheit

  C) Celsius degree

  D) Milligram

- What is the unit of measurement for molar concentration? (　　)

  A) Mol per liter

  B) Liter

  C) Gram

  D) Milligram

- What is the unit of measurement for atomic mass? (　　)

  A) Gram

  B) Kilogram

  C) Atomic mass unit

  D) Mole

- What is the unit of measurement for parts per million (ppm)? (　　)

  A) Liter

  B) Gram

  C) Milligram

  D) Mol per liter

- What is the unit of measurement for molar fraction? (　　)

  A) Mol per liter

  B) Molarity

  C) Liter

  D) None of the above

朗读二维码

1.2　Numbers and Mathematical Expressions

Numbers and mathematical expressions are essential in the study of chemistry and chemical engineering. They are used to quantify physical properties of substances, describe chemical reactions, and model complex systems. In this section, we will discuss the different types of numbers and mathematical expressions used in chemistry and chemical engineering.

(1) Arabic and Roman Numbers

As depicted in Table 1-1, there are two main types of numbers used in chemistry and chemical engineering: Arabic and Roman numbers. Arabic numbers (1, 2, 3...) are used for counting and for representing quantities. Roman numbers (Ⅰ, Ⅱ, Ⅲ...) are used for representing the elements of the periodic table, as well as for indicating the oxidation state of elements in chemical compounds.

Table 1-1 Arabic and Roman Numbers

Arabic numbers	Roman numbers	Arabic numbers	Roman numbers	Arabic numbers	Roman numbers
1	Ⅰ	11	XI	111	CXI
2	Ⅱ	20	XX	200	CC
3	Ⅲ	30	XXX	300	CCC
4	Ⅳ	40	XL	400	CD
5	Ⅴ	50	L	500	D
6	Ⅵ	60	LX	600	DC
7	Ⅶ	70	LXX	700	DCC
8	Ⅷ	80	LXXX	800	DCCC
9	Ⅸ	90	XC	900	CM
10	Ⅹ	100	C	1000	M

(2) Integers

Integers are whole numbers that do not have a fractional or decimal component. They can be positive, negative, or zero. Integers are used to represent quantities such as the number of atoms or molecules in a substance.

(3) Natural Numbers

Natural numbers are positive integers that are used to count objects. They start from one and continue indefinitely. Natural numbers are used to represent the number of particles in a system or the number of moles of a substance.

(4) Even and Odd Numbers

Even numbers are integers that are divisible by two, while odd numbers are integers that are not divisible by two. Even and odd numbers are used to describe the parity of particles or molecules in a system.

(5) Numerals

Numerals are symbols used to represent numbers. As shown in Table 1-2, numerals are used to indicate the number of atoms or functional groups in a molecule or compound.

Table 1-2   Commonly used numerals

1	单	mono-	6	六	hexa-	11	十一	undeca-
2	双	di-(bi-)	7	七	hepta-	12	十二	dodeca-
3	三	tri-	8	八	octa-	20	二十	icosa-
4	四	tetra-	9	九	nona-	100	百	hecta-
5	五	penta-	10	十	deca-	聚	多个	poly-

(6) Fractions and Decimals

Fractions and decimals are used to represent parts of a whole. Fractions are written as one number over another (e.g., 1/2), while decimals are written as a decimal point followed by a number (e.g., 0.5). Fractions and decimals are used to represent concentrations, percentages, and other physical properties of substances.

Examples:
- 1/2 -- one-half
- 1/3 -- one-third
- 1/4 -- a quarter, one-fourth
- 1/199 -- one over one hundred ninety-nine
- $1/C_A$ -- one over C sub A
- $C_A = t / (t + 1)$ -- C sub A equals t over t plus one
- 0.1 -- zero point one
- 0.01 -- zero point zero one

(7) Exponents

Exponents are used to represent repeated multiplication of a number by itself. They are written as a base number raised to a power (e.g., $3^2 = 9$). Exponents are used to represent the number of molecules in a substance, the rate of a chemical reaction, and other physical properties of substances.

Examples:
- 6^3 -- six cubed / six to the third
- 3^{-6} -- three to the minus sixth
- e^2 -- e squared / e to the second
- exp10 -- the exponential of 10
- $\exp(-E_a/RT)$ -- the exponential of minus E sub a over R times T
- 6.022×10^{23} -- six point zero two two multiplied by 10 to the twenty third

(8) Logarithms

Logarithms are used to represent the power to which a base number must be raised to produce a given number. They are written as log $_{(base)}$ (number) (e.g., $\log_{10}100$ = lg100 = 2). Logarithms are used to represent pH, pK_a, and other physical properties of substances.

Examples:
- lg1 = 0 -- log one equals zero
- $t = \lg[-1/(1+C_A)]$ -- t equals log minus one over one plus C sub A

(9) Formula

A mathematical expression used to describe a relationship between variables. For example, the formula for the volume of a cylinder is $V = \pi r^2 h$, where V is the volume, r is the radius, and h is the height.

Examples:
- Addition: 1+2 = 3 -- One plus two equals three.
- Subtraction: 3−2 = 1 -- Three minus two equals one.
- Multiplication: 1 × 2 = 2 -- One multiplied by two equals two. One times two equals two.
- Division: 2 ÷ 2 = 1 -- Two divided by 2 equals 1; 6 ÷ 2 × 3+1 = 10 -- Six divided by two multiplied by three plus one equals ten; 6 ÷ (2 × 3) +1 = 2 -- Six divided by round bracket two times three round bracket plus one equals two.
- Inequality: a < b -- a is less than b; a > b -- a is greater than b; a ≥ b -- a is less than or equal to b; a ≈ b -- a is approximately equal to b; a ≠ b -- a is not equal to b.
- √ -- the square root.
- ∑ -- the sum.

(10) Differentiation and Integration

Differentiation and integration are two fundamental mathematical operations used in chemical engineering. Differentiation is used to find the rate of change of a variable, while integration is used to find the area under a curve. These operations are used in areas such as reaction kinetics and process control.

Examples:

- $d(ax)/dx = a$ -- d a x d x equals a.
- $-r_A = dC_A/dt$ -- minus r sub A equals d C sub A d t.
- $d(ax^n)/dx = anx^n$ -- d a times x to the nth d x equals a times n times x to the n minus 1.
- $\int ax dx = a$ -- The integral of a times x d x equals a.
- $\int_b^c ax dx = c-b$ -- The integral of a times x d x from b to c equals c minus b.

Conclusion

Numbers and mathematical expressions are essential in chemistry and chemical engineering. They are used to represent physical properties of substances, describe chemical reactions, and model complex systems. Understanding the different types of numbers and mathematical expressions used in chemistry is essential for anyone studying or working in the field.

朗读二维码

专业词汇

- numbers　数字
- Arabic number　阿拉伯数字
- Roman number　罗马数字
- integer　整数
- natural number　自然数
- positive number　正数
- negative number　负数
- even number　偶数
- odd number　奇数
- numeral　数字
- fraction　分数
- decimal number　十进制数
- exponent　指数
- logarithm　对数

- natural logarithm 自然对数
- common logarithm 常用对数
- formula 公式
- addition 加法
- subtraction 减法
- multiplication 乘法
- division 除法
- equality 等式
- inequality 不等式
- differentiation 微分
- integration 积分

常用句型

- Exponents **are used to** represent repeated multiplication of a number by itself. 指数用来表示一个数与它本身的重复乘法。

【句型解释】该句型中的主要词汇包括 exponents、represent、repeated multiplication、number 和 itself。科技英语中使用"**be used to**"这个句型时，可以用来说明某个数学概念或原理的作用及其具体含义。

【例句】In thermodynamics, the exponent of a temperature term **is used to** describe the relationship between temperature and the rate of a chemical reaction. 在热力学中，温度项的指数用于描述温度和化学反应速率之间的关系。

互动练习

【英译中】The addition symbol "+" represents the addition of two numbers.____

【英译中】In the equation $y = 2x - 5$, y represents the vertical axis and x represents the horizontal axis.____

【中译英】一百减去五十等于五十。____

【中译英】这个算式是五加上七再乘以三。____

【中译英】π 是一个无限不循环小数，约等于 3.14。____

- Which type of number is used to represent the elements of the periodic table? ( )

  A) Arabic numbers

  B) Roman numbers

  C) Integers

  D) Natural numbers

- Which mathematical expression is used to represent repeated multiplication of a number by itself? ( )

  A) Exponents

  B) Logarithms

  C) Differentiation

  D) Integration

- Which type of number is used to represent the number of particles in a system or the number of moles of a substance? ( )

  A) Arabic numbers

  B) Roman numbers

  C) Integers

  D) Natural numbers

- Which mathematical operation is used to find the rate of change of a variable? ( )

  A) Exponents

  B) Logarithms

  C) Differentiation

  D) Integration

- Which mathematical expression is used to describe a relationship between variables? ( )

  A) Exponents

  B) Logarithms

  C) Formula

  D) Integration

1.3 Graphics and Charts

Graphics and charts are essential tools for presenting data in a visual format, making it easier to understand and analyze. In this section, we will discuss the different types of graphics and charts, their dimensions, and the specialized vocabulary used to describe them.

(1) Dimensions

Graphics and charts can be classified according to their dimensions, which can be one-dimensional, two-dimensional, or three-dimensional. One-dimensional graphics are rectilinear, meaning they consist of straight lines; while two-dimensional graphics are rounded, meaning they consist of curves. Three-dimensional graphics as depicted in Figure 1-6 are stereoscopic, meaning they have depth and appear to be three-dimensional.

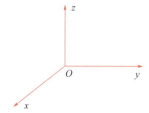

Figure 1-6 3D coordinate diagram

(2) Planar and Steric Forms

Planar forms are two-dimensional shapes that lie flat on a surface, such as a triangle, quadrangle, square, pentagon, hexagon, or circle. Steric forms, on the other hand, are three-dimensional shapes, such as a cube, regular tetrahedron, octahedron, triangular pyramid, square pyramid, or sphere. Figure 1-7 shows some images of them.

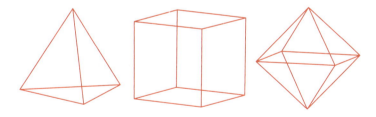

Figure 1-7 Triangular pyramid, cube and octahedron

(3) Specialized Vocabulary

When working with graphics and charts, it is important to understand the specialized vocabulary used to describe them. For example, the vertical axis is also known as the y-axis, while the horizontal axis is the x-axis. A bar graph is a type of chart that uses bars to represent data as depicted in Figure 1-8, while a line graph uses lines to connect data points. A fan-shaped graph as shown in Figure 1-9 is a type of pie chart that represents data as a proportion of a circle.

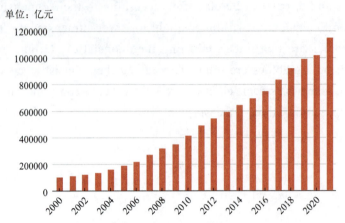

Figure 1-8　Changes in China's GDP from 2000 to 2020 (bar graph)

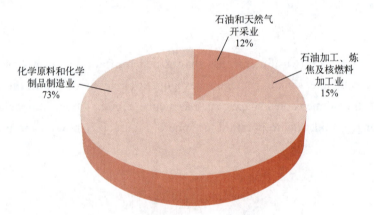

Figure 1-9　Proportion of fixed assets investment in three sub industries of the petrochemical industry from January to August 2017 (fan-shaped graph)

（4）Functions

Functions are mathematical expressions that describe the relationship between two variables. In graphics and charts, functions can be used to represent data. A proportion function represents data that is directly proportional, while an inversely proportion function represents data that is inversely proportional. An exponent function represents data that follows an exponential growth pattern, while a logarithm function represents data that follows a logarithmic growth pattern.

Conclusion

Graphics and charts are essential tools in the field of chemistry and other industries. Understanding the dimensions of graphics and charts, as well as the specialized vocabulary used to describe them, is important for effectively presenting data in a visual format. Additionally, understanding functions and how they can be used to represent data is essential for accurately interpreting graphics and charts.

专业词汇

朗读二维码

- dimension　维
- one dimension　一维
- two dimensions　二维
- rectilinear　直线的
- rounded　曲线的
- planar　平面的
- stereoscopic　立体的
- symmetric(al)　对称的
- asymmetric(al)　非对称的
- plane figure　平面图形
- triangle　三角形
- quadrangle　四角形
- square　正方形
- pentagon　五角形
- hexagon　六角形
- round　圆形
- steric form　立体图形
- cube　立方体
- regular tetrahedron　正四面体
- octahedron　八面体
- triangular pyramid　三角锥形
- square pyramid　四角锥形

Part 1 General English for Science and Technology

- sphere　球形
- vertical axis, *y*-axis　纵轴
- horizontal axis, *x*-axis　横轴
- bar graph　柱状图
- line graph　折线图
- fan-shaped graph　扇形图
- proportion function　比例函数
- inversely proportion function　反比例函数
- exponent function　指数函数
- logarithm function　对数函数

常用句型

- A bar graph **is a type of** chart **that** uses bars to represent data as depicted in Figure 1-8, while a line graph uses lines to connect data points. 柱状图是一种用柱形表示数据的图表（如图 1-8 所示），而折线图则用线条连接数据点。

  【句型解释】A bar graph **is a type of** chart 句型用于介绍某个事物或现象的类型，表示前者属于后者的一种类型，后者通常是一个更广泛的类别。**that** uses bars to represent data 句型描述前者具体的功能或特点。

  【例句】A mass spectrometry spectrum is **a type of** chart **that** shows the distribution of ions according to their mass-to-charge ratio. 质谱图谱是一种图形类型，它显示离子根据它们的质荷比分布的情况。

互动练习

- Which of the following statements is true regarding one-dimensional graphics?
  (　　)
  A) They consist of curves
  B) They are stereoscopic
  C) They lie flat on a surface
  D) They consist of straight lines
- What is the specialized vocabulary used to describe the vertical axis of a chart?
  (　　)
  A) The *x*-axis
  B) The *y*-axis

C) The *z*-axis

D) The *a*-axis

- Which of the following is a steric form? (　　)

    A) Triangle

    B) Circle

    C) Cube

    D) Pentagon

- What type of chart uses bars to represent data? (　　)

    A) Pie chart

    B) Line graph

    C) Bar graph

    D) Fan-shaped graph

- Which function represents data that follows a logarithmic growth pattern? (　　)

    A) Proportion function

    B) Inversely proportion function

    C) Exponent function

    D) Logarithm function

Exercises

【Speak & Listen】场景：两位学生在化学实验室里做实验，他们正在讨论实验过程中使用到的单位和数值表述。

A: Hey, have you measured the volume of this solution yet?

B: Yeah, I used a graduated cylinder and got 50 milliliters.

A: Wait, what? Did you say 50 or 15?

B: 50, I'm sure. Don't worry, I can convert it to liters for you. It's 0.05 liters.

A: Oh, thanks. And what's the concentration of this solution?

B: It's 0.1 molar, or 0.1 moles per liter.

A: Got it. And what about the temperature?

B: It's around 25 degrees Celsius, but we need to convert it to Kelvin for our calculations.

A: Why do we need to do that?

B: Because most chemical equations require temperature to be expressed in Kelvin. It's just a simple conversion though, just add 273 to get the Kelvin temperature.

A: Okay, got it. Wait, why are you drawing a graph of our data?

B: Because it's easier to visualize the relationship between our variables. Plus, it looks cool!

A: Haha, yeah you're right. Speaking of cool, have you seen the latest edition of our chemistry textbook?

B: Yeah, it's so cool that they added a glossary of common chemical terms and symbols.

A: And the index is so helpful too! I found the section on chemical bonding in no time.

B: I know, right? It's a good thing we're studying chemistry, or we'd never understand all these units and symbols.

A: Yeah, I'm just glad we have each other to explain things to.

B: Me too, buddy. Now let's get back to our experiment before the professor catches us goofing off!

【Write & Read】分析某化工过程的温度变化趋势

训练内容：运用常用单位与表述、数字与数式、图形与图表的基础知识，撰写一份关于某化工过程温度变化趋势的报告。

Report on Temperature Changes in a Chemical Process

Introduction:

The purpose of this report is to analyze the temperature changes that occurred during a chemical process. The temperature was measured in Celsius (°C) every minute over the course of one hour.

Results:

The initial temperature was 25°C. The temperature then rose to 40°C in the first 10 minutes and stayed constant for the next 20 minutes. After that, the temperature started to decrease and reached 30°C in the next 10 minutes. In the last 20 minutes, the temperature decreased gradually and stabilized at 20°C.

Discussion:

The graph clearly shows the temperature changes over time. During the first 10 minutes, the temperature increased rapidly, indicating an exothermic reaction. The temperature then remained constant for the next 20 minutes, suggesting that the reaction had reached equilibrium. After 30 minutes, the temperature started to decrease, indicating that the reaction had become endothermic. The final temperature of 20°C suggests that the reaction had completed.

Conclusion

In conclusion, the temperature changes observed in the chemical process indicate that an exothermic reaction occurred initially, followed by a period of equilibrium and then an endothermic reaction. The final temperature of 20°C suggests that the reaction has completed. These results are consistent with what is expected in a chemical reaction, and they provide useful information for further investigation.

2 Literature English

搜一搜，
了解专业背景

化学文献结构
文献写作技巧讲解
实验结果展示方法

搜一搜，
获取学习资源

文献撰写视频教程
实验数据案例文档
实验结果案例图片
化学文献常用术语中英文对照

2.1 Components of General Literature

General scientific literature includes papers, patents, industry standards, operating procedures, and more. While the structures may vary, they usually include the title, author's name, organization name, abstract, text, appendix, etc.

(1) Title

The types of scientific literature in English are numerous, and a single technical journal (technical literature) will contain a large number of documents. The title is the first information that readers see and determines whether they want to read further. Therefore, the title should not only summarize the content of the literature but also be as concise as possible and leave a lasting impression on the reader.

Sometimes, the title includes a subtitle outside of the main theme, where the subject only states important and concise information, and the subtitle adds further explanation when necessary.

Commonly used language for the title includes "novel/new" "academic journal" "subject/theme/main topic" "subtitle" "interesting results/interesting findings" "format" "limitation" and "impact".

Example:

> Efficiency enhancement of polyfluorene:
> Polystyrene blend light-emitting diodes by
> simultaneous trap dilution and β-phase formation

(2) Author's Name

The author's name refers to the names of the members who conducted the research (technical development), usually arranged in order. In most cases, the name of the person who made the greatest contribution is listed first, followed by the names of the co-authors in descending order.

(3) Organization Name

The organization name refers to the institution, company, or laboratory that the author is affiliated with. It is generally listed below the author's name and is used to identify the author's research background.

Examples for Author's Name and Organization Name:

Elham Khodabakhshi, Paul W. M. Blom, (iD) **and Jasper J. Michels**[a] (iD)

AFFILIATIONS

Max Planck Institute for Polymer Research, Ackermannweg 10, 55128 Mainz, Germany

[a]michels@mpip-mainz.mpg.de

(4) Abstract

The abstract is a brief summary of the literature, and its main purpose is to provide readers with a general understanding of the content of the literature. It should be concise, accurate, and informative and should include the research purpose, methods, results, and conclusions.

Example:

ABSTRACT

By diluting poly(dioctylfluorene) (PFO) with low molecular weight polystyrene (PS), electron trapping and trap-assisted recombination can be strongly suppressed. For polymer light-emitting diodes (PLEDs) consisting of a PFO : PS (1 : 3) blend, a doubling of the efficiency is expected owing to trap dilution. Experimentally, we observe a much larger efficiency increase of nearly an order of magnitude. The electroluminescence and photoluminescence spectra of the PFO : PS blend show a sharpening of the vibrational peaks with regard to pristine PFO with the emission maximum at 436 nm. This spectral feature is characteristic of the formation of the β-phase in PFO upon PS addition.

（5）Text

The text is the main content of the literature, including the introduction, experimental section, results, discussion, and conclusion. It should be organized logically, and the arguments should be clear and coherent.

The experimental section is a detailed description of the methods used to conduct the research, including the materials, equipment, and procedures used. It should be comprehensive and accurate to ensure that the experiment can be repeated by others.

（6）Appendix

The appendix includes supplementary materials such as tables, graphs, and images, which provide additional information to support the arguments presented in the text.

Conclusion

In conclusion, scientific literature has a well-defined structure that includes a title, author's name, organization name, abstract, text, and appendix. Understanding the components of scientific literature is essential for researchers and anyone working in the scientific community.

朗读二维码

专业词汇

- novel / new　新型
- academic journal　学术杂志
- subject / theme / main topic　主题
- subtitle　副题
- interesting results / interesting findings　有趣的结果
- format　格式
- limitation　限制
- impact　影响
- author's name　著者名
- researcher　研究者

- first author / top name　第一作者
- corresponding author　通讯作者（研究责任者）
- affiliation　所属
- institution　设施
- university / college　大学
- department　学科
- research institute　研究所

常用句型

- The text is the main content of the literature, **including** the introduction, experimental section, results, discussion, and conclusion. 正文是文献的主要内容，包括引言、实验部分、结果、讨论和结论。

  【句型解释】此句型用于描述某文献或论文应包含的主要内容。在这个句型中，主句是"The text is the main content of the literature"；**including** 补充列举了具体内容："introduction, experimental section, results, discussion, and conclusion"。

  【例句】The research paper should include several sections, **including** an introduction, experimental section, results, discussion, and conclusion. 研究论文应包括几个部分，包括引言、实验部分、结果、讨论和结论。

互动练习

- What is the purpose of the abstract in scientific literature? (　　)
  A) To provide readers with a general understanding of the content of the literature
  B) To list the author's name and organization name
  C) To include supplementary materials such as tables and graphs
  D) To provide a detailed description of the methods used to conduct the research
- What should the title of a scientific literature accomplish? (　　)
  A) Summarize the content of the literature
  B) Be as long as possible to include all important information
  C) Use only general terms to avoid confusion
  D) Include the author's name and organization name
- What is the purpose of the experimental section in scientific literature? (　　)

A) To provide a brief summary of the literature

B) To list the materials and equipment used in the research

C) To organize the arguments clearly and coherently

D) To provide a detailed description of the methods used to conduct the research

- What is included in the appendix of scientific literature? (　　)

  A) The main content of the literature, including introduction, experimental section, results, discussion, and conclusion

  B) A brief summary of the literature

  C) Supplementary materials such as tables, graphs, and images

  D) The research purpose, methods, results, and conclusions

- What is the importance of understanding the components of scientific literature? (　　)

  A) It helps researchers conduct better experiments

  B) It allows readers to identify the author's research background

  C) It enables researchers to communicate their findings effectively

  D) It is essential for anyone working in the scientific community

朗读二维码

2.2 Main Components and Common Terms of the Body Text

The body text is the main part of a document and the most important section. It includes the motivation and value of scientific research or technological development, the description of experimental results, and the conclusion logically derived from the experimental results.

(1) Motivation and Value

Scientific research or technological development is aimed at solving problems or answering questions, which is the motivation behind it. This motivation may come from intuition or insight, which is often the result of previous research and learning. Therefore, when introducing the motivation of a document, it is necessary to describe the research situation of other documents that lead to the research motivation, which is usually the first half of the introduction of the document.

Moreover, any scientific research or technological development is a part of a certain discipline (technical field). Therefore, in the document, it is necessary to elaborate on the role and position of the scientific research or technological development in the entire field, that is, the research value, which is usually the second half of the introduction of the document.

(2) Description of Experimental Results

The description of experimental results is usually after the introduction (or sometimes at the end of the document). In the description of experimental results, it is necessary to describe the part of the experimental data that can logically deduce the final conclusion of the document. The purpose of describing factual data is to convince all readers of the conclusion of the document with concise and clear language. If this part of the content is ambiguous, the credibility of the entire document will be greatly reduced.

If the theme of the document involves the discovery of new materials, in order to determine the structure of the new materials, various spectra must be provided and demonstrated to be different from similar materials. If the discovery of a new reaction is involved, in order to determine the reaction mechanism, intermediate extraction and determination, reaction kinetics testing, and thermodynamics testing must be carried out to obtain the necessary data to support the conclusion.

(3) Conclusion

After the various collections and analyses of experimental results, the conclusion of the document can be derived. Different conclusions have different modes of expression:

- The same experimental result A logically deduces conclusion B or multiple non-contradictory conclusions B and C.

Typical sentence pattern: Based on the experimental result(s) A, it is clearly concluded to B and C.

- Multiple experimental results A and B support a conclusion C.

Typical sentence pattern: The experimental results A and B can doubtlessly reveal the conclusion ofC.

- Several experimental results A logically deduce a certain conclusion a, while other experimental results B logically deduce another conclusion b. Multiple conclusions reveal a deeper conclusion c together.

Typical sentence pattern: The experimental results A show the fact a, and another one B exhibits the case of b. Consequently, considering all these findings, we can conclude c.

朗读二维码

专业词汇

- motivation　动机
- experimental results　实验结果
- logically　逻辑上
- conclusion　结论
- sense　感觉
- intuition　直觉
- part　部分
- progress report　进展报告
- new material　新材料
- structure　结构
- spectra　光谱
- evidence　证据
- verification　验证
- proof　证明
- demonstration　展示
- prove　证实
- show　展示
- confirm　确认
- certify　证明
- verify　核实
- new reaction　新反应
- reaction mechanism　反应机理
- intermediate　中间体
- reaction kinetics　反应动力学
- thermodynamics　热力学

常用句型

- Based on the experimental result(s) A, **it is clearly concluded to** B and C. 根据实验结果 A，可以明确提出 B 和 C 的结论。

  【句型解释】该句型用于表达一项实验结果 A，可以明确得出结论 B 和 C。其中，**it is clearly concluded** 强调结论的明确性，使用被动语态突出结论的客观性和确定性。

【例句】Based on the experimental results, **it is clearly concluded** that the reaction rate increases with temperature and concentration. 基于实验结果，可以明确得出结论：反应速率随温度和浓度升高而增加。

互动练习

- What is the purpose of the introduction in a scientific document? (　　)
  A) To describe the experimental results
  B) To provide a conclusion
  C) To elaborate on the role and position of the research in the entire field
  D) To demonstrate the spectra of new materials
- What is the purpose of providing factual data in a scientific document? (　　)
  A) To increase the length of the document
  B) To make the document more interesting
  C) To convince readers of the conclusion with concise and clear language
  D) To confuse readers
- What is required to determine the reaction mechanism when a new reaction is discovered? (　　)
  A) Experimental results A and B
  B) Intermediate extraction and determination
  C) Reaction kinetics testing
  D) Thermodynamics testing
- What is the sentence pattern typically used when different experimental results logically deduce multiple non-contradictory conclusions? (　　)
  A) The experimental results A and B can doubtlessly reveal the conclusion of C
  B) The experimental results A show the fact a, and another one B exhibits the case of b. Consequently, considering all these findings, we can conclude to c
  C) Based on the experimental result(s) A, it is clearly concluded to B (B and C)
  D) None of the above
- What is the purpose of the conclusion in a scientific document? (　　)
  A) To describe the experimental results
  B) To provide a new hypothesis
  C) To convince readers of the research motivation
  D) To derive a conclusion logically from the experimental results

2.3 Presentation and Common Terms in Experimental Results

The experimental section of a research paper is crucial to ensure the reproducibility of the results. In other words, if the same experimental protocol is followed by anyone, anywhere, at any time, they should obtain nearly identical results. If experimental results cannot be reproduced, they will not be recognized by the scientific community, unless there is an inherent randomness in the nature of the phenomenon being studied. Therefore, the experimental section must clearly describe the implementation of the reaction, the analytical instruments and methods used, and any special reagents that were utilized.

During chemical reactions, crude products are often obtained as mixtures of main products, byproducts, and unreacted starting materials. Therefore, it is essential to describe the methods used to purify the compounds by removing impurities in the experimental results section.

(1) Essential Records Related to Reactants

When recording the reaction operation, it is necessary to document the amount (mass, moles), temperature, pressure, solvent type, concentration, and presence of a catalyst, among other important conditions.

Example:

> **Materials.** 1,4-Bis(hexyloxy)benzene was prepared by the reported procedure. $Bu_3PPd(Ph)Br$ (2) and 2-(7-bromo-9,9-dioctyl-9H-fluoren-2-yl)-4,4,5,5-tetramethyl-1,3,2-dioxa-borolane (3) were prepared according to the established procedures.[49] Dry tetrahydrofran (THF) and other reagents were commercial products and were used without further purification.

(2) Record of Reaction Operations

After adding the reactants to the reaction vessel, they are usually mixed thoroughly by stirring, followed by heating or cooling to reach the desired temperature. The reaction is then allowed to proceed for a certain period. Sometimes, heating under reflux or light irradiation may also be required.

2 Literature English

Example:

> Synthesis of 1b. A flask was charged with glacial acetic acid (55 mL), H_2SO_4 (2 mL), water(9 mL), and CCl_4 (12 mL), and into the flask were added 1,4-bis (hexyloxy) benzene (5.04 g, 18.1 mmol), iodine (4.14 g, 16.3 mmol),and iodic acid (1.90 g, 10.8 mmol). The resulting mixture was heated at 70 ℃ for 24 h.

(3) Record of Separation Operations

After the reaction is complete, certain separation operations need to be carried out. This record is usually documented after the experimental process. The record should be as quantitative and concise as possible, clearly stating the required amount of reagent. Typical separation operations include filtration, crystallization, extraction, washing, recrystallization, distillation, vacuum distillation, fractional distillation, solvent evaporation, absorption, decolorization, and chromatographic separation.

Example:

> After this time, a solution of sodium was heated at 70℃ for 24 h. After this time, a solution of sodium thiosulfate was added to remove any unreacted iodine. The solution was extracted with diethyl ether and washed successively with 5% NaOH solution and water. The organic layer was dried over $MgSO_4$ and the solvent was removed under reduced pressure. Column chromatography on silica gel with hexane, followed by recrystallization from hexane, afforded 1,4-bis(hexyloxy)-2,5-diodobenzene as a white powder (4.67 g, 49%); melting point 54.2-55.0 ℃.

(4) Recording of Product Data

After the refinement and separation processes, data related to the products should be recorded, including product yield, melting point(m.p.) or boiling point(b.p.), and spectroscopic data.

Example:

> white powder (4.67 g, 49%); m.p. 54.2-55.0 ℃. IR (KBr): 2950, 2918, 2857, 1450, 1213, 849.526 cm^{-1}. ^1H NMR (500 MHz, $CDCl_3$) δ: 7.17 (s, 2 H), 3.93 (t. $J = 6.5$ Hz, 4 H), 1.80 (quint, $J = 6.5$ Hz, 4 H), 1.53-1.47 (m, 4 H),

1.37-1.32 (m, 8 H), 0.91 (t, J =7.0 Hz, 6 H). ^{13}C NMR (126 MHz, CDCl$_3$) δ: 152.8, 122.7, 86.3, 70.3, 31.5, 29.1, 25.7, 22.6, 14.0.

Conclusion

In summary, this section highlights the importance of accurately recording and reporting experimental data in chemical reactions. The inclusion of necessary information ensures that the results are reproducible, reliable, and can be effectively communicated in scientific literature.

朗读二维码

专业词汇

- reproducibility　再现性
- memo　记录
- notation　符号表示
- note　注释
- record　记录
- accident　偶然事件
- reaction　反应
- analytical instrument　分析仪器
- analytical method　分析方法
- raw material　原料
- crude product　粗生成物
- main product　主产物 / principal product　主产物
- by-product　副产物
- unreacted substance　未反应物
- mixture　混合物
- purification　精制
- isolation　分离

- impurity 不纯物
- pure substance 纯物质
- reactant 反应物
- catalyst 催化剂
- reaction container 反应容器
- stirring 搅拌
- heating temperature 加热温度
- cooling temperature 冷却温度
- reaction time 反应时间
- reflux by heating 加热回流
- light irradiation 光照射
- experimental procedure 实验流程
- quantitative 定量的
- filtration 过滤
- crystallization 结晶
- extraction 萃取
- washing 洗涤
- recrystallization 重结晶
- distillation 蒸馏
- reduced pressure distillation 减压蒸馏
- fractional distillation 分馏
- distillation of solvent 蒸馏溶剂
- adsorption 吸附
- bleach 脱色
- column chromatography 层析柱分离
- yield 收率
- melting point (m.p.) 熔点
- boiling point (b.p.) 沸点
- data 数据

常用句型

- **In other words**, if the same experimental protocol is followed by anyone, anywhere, at any time, they should obtain nearly identical results. 换句话说，如果任何人在任何时间、任何地点遵循相同的实验方案，都会得到几乎相同的结果。

Part 1 General English for Science and Technology

【句型解释】本句为条件状语从句，用来描述在某种条件下结果会如何。句型结构为："**In other words**, if + 条件 1, 条件 2, 条件 3, then + 结果"。本句含义为"换言之，如果满足条件 1、条件 2、条件 3，那么结果 A 应该 / 将会……"，常用于科技文献中概括或进一步解释某个现象或结果的原因或必要性。**In other words** 表示"换句话说"或"也就是说"，用于重新表述之前的内容，使其更清楚或更容易理解。

【例句】**In other words**, if impurities are not removed during the purification process, then the characterization of the final product will be inaccurate. 换句话说，在纯化过程中如果未能去除杂质，那么最终产物的表征将会不准确。

互动练习

【英译中】In other words, if the concentration of the reagent is too low, then the reaction rate will be significantly reduced._____

_____

- What is the purpose of the experimental section in a research paper? (　　)
    A) To provide background information on the topic
    B) To describe the implementation of the reaction and analytical instruments
    C) To present the results obtained from the experiment
    D) To discuss the implications of the findings
- Why is it important to describe the methods used to purify compounds in the experimental results section? (　　)
    A) To make the paper longer
    B) To impress the readers
    C) To ensure that the results are reproducible
    D) To increase the yield of the reaction
- What information should be documented when recording the reaction operation? (　　)
    A) The author's name
    B) The reaction color
    C) The temperature and pressure
    D) The research topic
- What is the purpose of separation operations in chemical reactions? (　　)
    A) To create byproducts
    B) To remove impurities from the product
    C) To increase the yield of the reaction

D) To add catalysts to the reaction
- What data related to the products should be recorded after the refinement and separation processes? (   )

  A) The author's name

  B) The color of the product

  C) The yield and melting or boiling point

  D) The name of the solvent used

Exercises

【Speak & Listen】图书馆里的对话

A: Hey, have you finished your research paper on polymers?

B: Not yet, I'm still struggling with the literature review part.

A: Ah, the most exciting part! You know what? I heard a rumor that the author of one of the articles you need to read is actually a unicorn(独角兽).

B: A unicorn? Really? That sounds like a joke.

A: I'm not kidding. It says right here in the article that the lead author's name is "Sparkles the Unicorn."

B: (laughs) Okay, I guess I'll have to read that one first. But what about the other sources?

A: Well, you could try reading the one that's written entirely in emojis. It's about the use of catalytic converters in the auto industry.

B: (laughs) That sounds like a fun challenge. I could use a break from all the technical jargon(行话).

A: Exactly! And if you need a break from reading, there's always the option of looking at some graphs and charts. I hear they're great for a mid-study nap.

B: (laughs) I'll keep that in mind. Thanks for the tips.

A: No problem. And remember, if you get too stressed out, just imagine that you're a molecule floating peacefully in a solution.

B: (laughs) I'll definitely try that. Thanks for making the library a little more fun.

A: Anytime. Good luck with your paper!

搜一搜，
检验学习效果

- 化学文献常用术语的英文测试选择题
- 化学实验数据展示英文讨论

【Write & Read】写一篇关于制备某一化学品的实验报告，包括实验目的、方法、结果和结论。

Preparation of Carbon Dioxide

Abstract

The experiment aimed to prepare carbon dioxide by reacting calcium carbonate and hydrochloric acid in a gas generator. The carbon dioxide produced was collected using a gas syringe and tested for its properties.

Introduction

The objective of this experiment is to prepare and collect carbon dioxide gas by the reaction between calcium carbonate and hydrochloric acid.

Methodology

The apparatus used for this experiment was a gas generator containing calcium carbonate and hydrochloric acid. As the reaction proceeded, the carbon dioxide produced was collected using a gas syringe. The gas was then tested for its properties. To test for the presence of carbon dioxide, the collected gas was bubbled through limewater. If carbon dioxide is present, a white precipitate of calcium carbonate is formed.

Results

The reaction between calcium carbonate and hydrochloric acid produced a gas which was collected in the gas syringe. When the gas was bubbled through limewater, a white precipitate of calcium carbonate was formed, indicating the presence of carbon dioxide. The gas also showed acidic properties when passed over moist blue litmus paper, which turned red.

Conclusion

The experiment was successful in preparing carbon dioxide by reacting calcium carbonate and hydrochloric acid. The collected gas was tested for its properties, which showed the presence of carbon dioxide and its acidic nature. The experiment demonstrated the basic principles of gas preparation and collection ,as well as the properties of carbon dioxide.

Part 2

Specialized English for Chemistry and Chemical Engineering

　　化学化工，其内涵通常被概括为"五大化学"（无机化学、有机化学、分析化学、物理化学、高分子化学）和"三传一反"（动量传递工程、热量传递工程、质量传递工程、化学反应工程）。

　　让学生系统化地了解化学、化工过程的概念和设备的英语表达，是本部分内容的设置目的。

3

Basics of Chemistry

搜一搜，
了解专业背景

无机化学都讲了些什么？
有机化学都讲了些什么？
分析化学都讲了些什么？
物理化学都讲了些什么？
高分子化学都讲了些什么？

搜一搜，
获取学习资源

无机化学的介绍视频
有机化学的介绍视频
分析化学的介绍视频
物理化学的介绍视频
高分子化学的介绍视频

3.1　Inorganic Chemistry

Inorganic chemistry is the branch of chemistry that deals with the study of elements and their compounds, excluding organic compounds that contain carbon-hydrogen bonds. Inorganic chemistry principles are crucial for understanding the behavior and properties of inorganic compounds and their applications in various fields such as materials science, environmental science, and chemical industries.

（1）Elemental Properties

Elements are substances that cannot be broken down into simpler substances by chemical means. Inorganic chemistry principles involve the study of the properties of elements, such as atomic structure, electronic configuration, and periodic trends, which are crucial for understanding their reactivity and behavior.

（2）Chemical Bonding

Chemical bonding is the interaction between atoms that results in the formation of a molecule or compound. Inorganic chemistry principles involve the study of various types of chemical bonding, such as ionic bonding (shown in Figure 3-1), covalent bonding (shown in Figure 3-2), and metallic bonding (shown in Figure 3-3), and their effects on the properties and behavior of inorganic compounds.

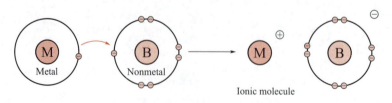

Figure 3-1　Ionic bond

3 Basics of Chemistry

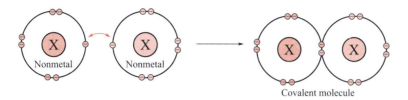

Figure 3-2　Covalent bond

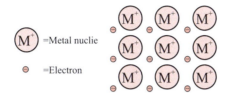

Figure 3-3　Metallic bond

(3) Acid-Base Chemistry

Acid-base chemistry involves the study of the behavior of acids and bases, including their reactions. Inorganic chemistry principles involve studying various types of acids and bases, their strengths and weaknesses, and their reactions with other compounds.

(4) Redox Reactions

As depicted in Figure 3-4, redox reactions involve the transfer of electrons between reactants. Inorganic chemistry principles involve the study of redox reactions and their applications in various fields, such as electrochemistry, corrosion, and energy storage.

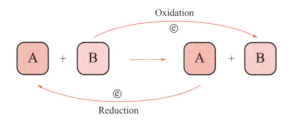

Figure 3-4　Redox reaction

(5) Applications

Inorganic chemistry principles have a wide range of applications in various fields, such as materials science, environmental science, and chemical industries. Some of the applications are:

- Synthesis and characterization of inorganic materials, such as ceramics, glasses, and metals;
- Environmental remediation and pollution control, such as wastewater treatment and air pollution control;
- Design and development of catalysts for various chemical reactions;
- Electrochemical energy storage and conversion, such as batteries and fuel cells.

Conclusion

Inorganic chemistry principles are crucial for understanding the behavior and properties of inorganic compounds and their applications in various fields. Understanding the properties of elements, chemical bonding, acid-base chemistry, and redox reactions is crucial for anyone working in these fields. Advances in inorganic chemistry continue to drive innovation and progress in various industries.

朗读二维码

专业词汇

- inorganic chemistry 无机化学
- atomic structure 原子结构
- electronic configuration 电子构造
- periodic trend 周期性趋势
- ionic bond 离子键
- covalent bond 共价键
- metallic bond 金属键
- acid 酸
- base 碱
- redox reactions 氧化还原反应
- electrochemistry 电化学
- corrosion 腐蚀
- energy storage 储能

3 Basics of Chemistry

常用句型

- Inorganic chemistry principles **involve the study of** redox reactions and their applications in various fields, such as electrochemistry, corrosion, and energy storage. 无机化学原理涉及氧化还原反应的研究及其在电化学、腐蚀和储能等各个领域的应用。

【句型解释】**involve the study of** 表达的意思是"……涉及对……的研究。"这个句型可以用来描述各种科学原理的研究领域和内容。

【例句】The synthesis and characterization of new inorganic materials **involve the study of** various types of chemical bonding, such as the formation of covalent bonds between atoms of different elements. 合成和表征新型无机材料涉及对各种类型的化学键的研究，例如不同元素的原子之间形成的共价键。

互动练习

- What is inorganic chemistry？（　　）
  A) The study of organic compounds containing carbon-hydrogen bonds
  B) The study of the properties and behavior of inorganic compounds
  C) The study of chemical reactions involving carbon-hydrogen bonds
  D) The study of chemical reactions involving only organic compounds
- What is chemical bonding？（　　）
  A) The interaction between atoms that results in the formation of a molecule or compound
  B) The study of the properties of elements
  C) The study of acids and bases
  D) The transfer of electrons between reactants
- What is acid-base chemistry？（　　）
  A) The study of various types of chemical bonding
  B) The study of redox reactions
  C) The study of the behavior of acids and bases and their reactions
  D) The study of the properties of inorganic compounds
- What are some applications of inorganic chemistry？（　　）
  A) Synthesis and characterization of organic materials
  B) Design and development of biological catalysts
  C) Environmental remediation and pollution control

D) Study of the behavior of organic compounds
- What is the importance of inorganic chemistry? (   )

  A) It helps in understanding the behavior and properties of inorganic compounds

  B) It helps in the study of organic compounds

  C) It helps in the study of biological systems

  D) It has no applications in any fields

朗读二维码

3.2　Organic Chemistry

Organic chemistry is the study of carbon-based compounds and their reactions. It is a fundamental field of chemistry with wide-ranging applications in industry, medicine, and materials science. In this section, we will discuss the basic principles of organic chemistry and their applications in different fields.

(1) Structure of Organic Compounds

Organic compounds are compounds that contain carbon atoms bonded to other elements, such as hydrogen, oxygen, nitrogen, and sulfur. The structure of organic compounds is determined by the number and arrangement of carbon atoms and their functional groups. Functional groups are groups of atoms that have specific chemical and physical properties and give organic compounds their characteristic reactivity.

(2) Bonding and Molecular Orbitals

The bonding in organic compounds is mainly covalent (shown in Figure 3-2), with carbon atoms forming four covalent bonds to other atoms. The bonding between carbon and other elements is influenced by their electronegativity and the hybridization of the carbon atom's orbitals. Molecular orbitals are the mathematical description of the distribution of electrons in a molecule, and they determine the molecule's reactivity and properties.

(3) Reactions of Organic Compounds

As shown in Figure 3-5, organic compounds can undergo a wide range of reactions, including substitution, elimination, addition, and rearrangement reactions. The reaction mechanism is determined by the nature of the functional groups and the type of reaction. Organic reactions are important in many fields, including medicine, materials science, and industry, where they are used to synthesize new compounds and modify existing ones.

3 Basics of Chemistry

Substitution

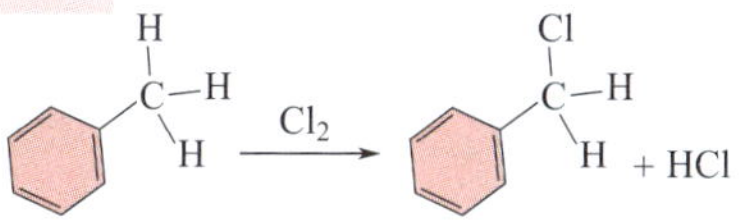

Addition

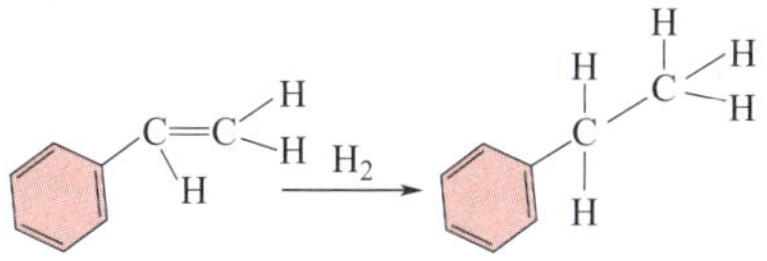

Elimination

$$C_6H_{12}O_6 \xrightarrow{H_2SO_4} 6C + 6H_2O$$

Rearrangement

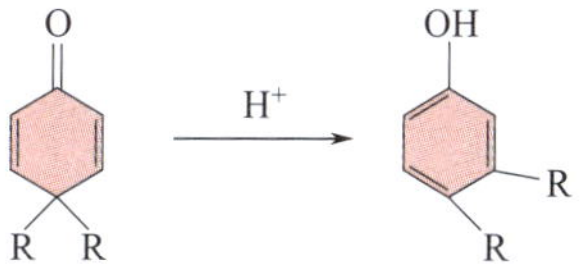

Figure 3-5　Types of organic reactions

(4) Applications

Organic chemistry has a wide range of applications in different fields. Some of the applications are:

- Drug discovery and development, where organic compounds are used as pharmaceuticals and chemical probes to study biological systems;
- Materials science, where organic compounds are used as building blocks for the synthesis of polymers, coatings, and electronic materials;
- Environmental chemistry, where organic compounds are studied for their impact on the environment and their role in chemical pollution;
- Industrial chemistry, where organic compounds are used as starting materials for synthesizing chemicals, such as plastics, dyes, and solvents.

Conclusion

Organic chemistry is a fundamental field with applications in industry, medicine, and materials science. Understanding the structure, bonding, and reactivity of organic compounds is crucial for anyone working in these fields. Advances in organic chemistry continue to drive the development of new materials and medicines and enhance our comprehension of the natural world.

专业词汇

朗读二维码

- organic chemistry　有机化学
- carbon-based compound　碳基化合物
- functional group　官能团
- characteristic reactivity　反应特性
- electronegativity　电负性
- hybridization　杂化性
- carbon atom's orbitals　碳原子轨道
- distribution of electrons　电子分布
- addition reaction　加成反应
- elimination reaction　消除反应
- substitution reaction　取代反应
- rearrangement reaction　重排反应
- biological system　生物系统

常用句型

- Drug discovery and development, where organic compounds **are used as** pharmaceuticals and chemical probes to study biological systems. 在药物发现和开发领域，有机化合物被用作药物和研究生物系统的化学探针。

【句型解释】此句型用于描述某种物质在某一领域的用途。结构为："物质 + **are used as** + 功能/用途 + in + 领域"。其中，"物质"指的是某种化学物质或材料；"功能/用途"说明该物质在该领域内的具体作用；"领域"则是应用的具体学科或行业。此句型可以清晰地表达物质的功能和应用场景。

【例句】Organic compounds **are used as** building blocks for the synthesis of polymers in materials science. 有机化合物在材料科学中被用作聚合物合成的基础单元。

互动练习

- What are functional groups in organic chemistry? (　　)
  A) Groups of atoms that give organic compounds their characteristic reactivity
  B) Groups of atoms that have no specific chemical or physical properties
  C) Groups of atoms that contain only hydrogen and carbon
  D) Groups of atoms that have a high electronegativity
- What determines the bonding between carbon and other elements in organic compounds? (　　)
  A) The size of the carbon atom's orbitals
  B) The shape of the carbon atom's orbitals
  C) The hybridization of the carbon atom's orbitals
  D) The electronegativity of the other elements
- Which of the following is NOT a type of reaction that organic compounds can undergo? (　　)
  A) Addition
  B) Elimination
  C) Subtraction
  D) Rearrangement
- What is one application of organic chemistry in materials science? (　　)
  A) Studying the impact of organic compounds on the environment
  B) Using organic compounds as pharmaceuticals and chemical probes
  C) Using organic compounds as building blocks for the synthesis of polymers
  D) Using organic compounds as starting materials for the synthesis of chemicals
- Why is understanding the structure, bonding, and reactivity of organic compounds important? (　　)
  A) It is important for the development of new materials and medicines.
  B) It is important for understanding the natural world.
  C) It is important for the synthesis of chemicals used in industry.
  D) All of the above.

3.3 Analytical Chemistry

朗读二维码

Analytical chemistry is the branch of chemistry that deals with the study of the chemical composition of substances and the determination of their quantities. In the chemical and process industries, analytical chemistry principles are crucial for quality control, process optimization, and product development. In this section, we will discuss the basic principles of analytical chemistry and their applications in the chemical and process industries.

(1) Chemical Properties

Chemical properties of substances determine their behavior in chemical reactions and their interactions with other substances. These properties include acidity, basicity, redox potential, and complexation ability. Understanding these properties is essential for the design of chemical processes, product development, and quality control.

(2) Analytical Methods

Analytical methods are techniques used to measure the chemical composition and quantity of substances. These methods include titration (as shown in Figure 3-6), spectrophotometry, chromatography, and electrochemistry. The choice of analytical method depends on the properties of the substance being analyzed and the required accuracy and precision.

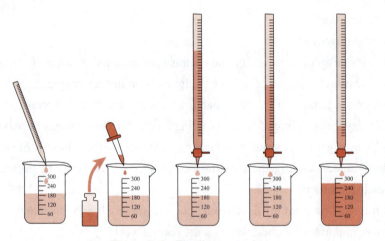

Figure 3-6 Titration procedure

(3) Calibration and Standardization

Calibration and standardization are essential for obtaining accurate and reliable analytical results. Calibration establishes a relationship between the analytical signal and the concentration of the analyte. Standardization involves the preparation of a reference material with a known concentration of the analyte.

（4）Applications

Analytical chemistry principles have a wide range of applications in the chemical and process industries. Some of the applications are:
- Quality control of raw materials, intermediates, and finished products;
- Process optimization and monitoring for efficient and sustainable production;
- Environmental monitoring for the detection and quantification of pollutants;
- Food and drug analysis for safety and regulatory compliance;
- Forensic analysis for the identification of substances and evidence.

Conclusion

Analytical chemistry principles are essential for the chemical and process industries, from quality control to product development and regulatory compliance. Understanding the chemical properties of substances, analytical methods, and calibration and standardization is crucial for anyone working in these industries. Advances in analytical chemistry are continuously improving the accuracy, precision, and speed of chemical analysis.

专业词汇

朗读二维码

- analytical chemistry　分析化学
- quality control　品质控制
- process optimization　工艺优化
- acidity　酸度
- basicity　碱度
- redox potential　氧化还原电位
- complexation ability　络合能力
- titration　滴定法
- spectrophotometry　分光光度法
- chromatography　色谱法
- accuracy　准确度
- precision　精密度

- calibration　校准
- standardization　标准化
- analyte　（被）分析物
- reference material　参比物
- environmental monitoring　环境监测
- regulatory compliance　法规遵从性
- forensic analysis　刑侦分析

常用句型

- Analytical methods **are techniques used to** measure the chemical composition and quantity of substances. 分析方法是用来测量物质的化学成分和数量的技术。

  【句型解释】这句话介绍了分析化学的意义，即分析方法是用来测量物质的化学成分和数量的技术手段。…… **is(are) technique(s) used to** ……常用来表示某学科（技术）的用途。

  【例句】In the pharmaceutical industry, high performance liquid chromatography (HPLC) i**s an analytical method used to** separate and quantify active pharmaceutical ingredients in drug formulations. 在制药业中，高效液相色谱法是一种用于分离和定量分析药物配方中的活性成分的方法。

互动练习

- What is analytical chemistry? (　　)
    A) The study of fluids and their behavior
    B) The study of chemical composition and determination of quantities
    C) The study of chemical reactions and their kinetics
    D) The study of atoms and molecules
- What are some chemical properties that determine the behavior of substances? (　　)
    A) Density, viscosity, and surface tension
    B) Acidity, basicity, and redox potential
    C) Mass, momentum, and energy
    D) Temperature, pressure, and composition
- Which of the following is NOT an analytical method? (　　)

A) Titration

B) Spectrophotometry

C) Mass spectrometry

D) Thermogravimetric analysis

- Why is calibration and standardization essential in analytical chemistry? (　　)

  A) To establish a relationship between the analytical signal and the concentration of the analyte

  B) To prepare a reference material with a known concentration of the analyte

  C) To ensure accurate and reliable analytical results

  D) All of the above

- What are some applications of analytical chemistry in the chemical and process industries? (　　)

  A) Transportation of fluids through pipelines

  B) Mixing and blending of fluids in chemical and food processing

  C) Quality control of raw materials, intermediates, and finished products

  D) None of the above

3.4 Physical Chemistry

朗读二维码

Physical chemistry is the branch of chemistry that deals with the study of the physical and chemical properties of matter, as well as the chemical reactions that occur between substances. In this section, we will discuss the basic principles of physical chemistry and their applications in various fields.

(1) Properties of Matter

Matter is anything that has mass and occupies space. The properties of matter, such as mass, volume, density, and specific heat capacity, determine their behavior when subjected to different forces.

Mass is the amount of matter in an object and is expressed in kilograms (kg). It is an important property for physical chemistry because it affects the amount of reactants and products in chemical reactions.

Volume is the amount of space occupied by an object and is expressed in cubic meters (m^3). It is an important property for physical chemistry because it affects the concentration and pressure of gases in chemical reactions.

Density is the mass per unit volume of a substance and is commonly expressed in kilograms per cubic meter (kg/m^3). It is an important property for physical chemistry because it affects the reaction rate and thermodynamic properties of substances.

Specific heat capacity (depicted in Figure 3-7) is the amount of heat required to raise the temperature of a substance by one degree Celsius and is expressed in joules per kilogram per degree Celsius [J/(kg·°C)]. It is an important property for physical chemistry because it affects the energy transfer in chemical reactions and the thermal stability of substances.

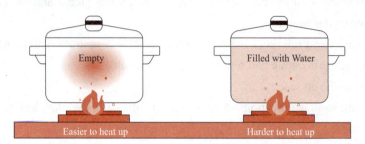

Figure 3-7　Specific heat capacity

(2) Thermodynamics

Thermodynamics deals with the study of energy and its transformations in chemical reactions and physical processes. The laws of thermodynamics are fundamental principles that govern the behavior of matter and energy.

The first law of thermodynamics states that energy cannot be created or destroyed, only transferred or converted from one to another. This law is important for physical chemistry because it relates to the energy balance in chemical reactions and processes.

The second law of thermodynamics states that the total entropy of a closed system can only increase or remain constant, but cannot decrease. This law is important for physical chemistry because it relates to the spontaneity and efficiency of chemical reactions and processes.

The third law of thermodynamics states that it is impossible to reach absolute zero temperature by any finite number of processes. This law is important for physical chemistry because it relates to the behavior of substances at low temperatures and the possibility of achieving perfect crystallization.

(3) Kinetics

Kinetics deals with the study of the rates and mechanisms of chemical reactions. The reaction rate is the change in concentration of a reactant or product per unit time and is affected by factors such as temperature, pressure, and catalysts.

The rate law is an expression that relates the reaction rate to the concentrations of the reactants and the order of the reaction. The activation energy is the energy required for a reaction to occur and is related to the reaction rate and the Arrhenius equation.

(4) Applications

Physical chemistry principles have a wide range of applications in various fields. Some of the applications are:
- Design and optimization of chemical processes for the production of chemicals, fuels, and materials;
- Development of new materials with specific properties, such as catalytic activity, electrical conductivity, and mechanical strength;
- Characterization of the thermodynamic and kinetic properties of substances, such as enthalpy, entropy, and reaction mechanisms;
- Control and optimization of reaction conditions, such as temperature, pressure, and catalysts, for increased yield and selectivity;
- Understanding and mitigating the environmental impact of chemical processes and materials.

Conclusion

Physical chemistry principles are essential for designing and optimizing chemical processes and materials in various fields. Understanding the properties of matter, thermodynamics, and kinetics is crucial for anyone working in these fields.

专业词汇

朗读二维码

- physical chemistry　物理化学
- mass　质量
- density　密度
- specific heat capacity　比热容
- thermodynamics　热力学
- entropy　熵
- spontaneity of chemical reactions and processes　化学反应和过程的自发性
- absolute zero temperature　绝对零度
- kinetics　动力学

- activation energy 活化能
- Arrhenius equation 阿伦尼乌斯方程
- enthalpy 焓

常用句型

- The properties of matter, such as mass, volume, density, and specific heat capacity, determine their behavior **when subjected to** different forces. 物质的质量、体积、密度和比热容等性质决定了它们在受到不同力作用时的行为。

【句型解释】"**when subjected to**"表示"受到……作用"，用于描述物质在某些条件或外力下的行为和反应。这个句型能够清晰传达出物质属性与其行为之间的因果关系，非常适用于物理化学领域的研究和描述。

【例句】The density and specific heat capacity of a substance determine its heat transfer and thermal stability **when subjected to** different temperatures and pressures. 物质的密度和比热容决定了它在不同温度和压力下的传热性和热稳定性。

互动练习

- Which of the following properties of matter affects the concentration and pressure of gases in chemical reactions? (　　)
  A) Mass
  B) Volume
  C) Density
  D) Specific heat capacity
- Which of the following laws of thermodynamics is related to the energy balance in chemical reactions and processes? (　　)
  A) First law of thermodynamics
  B) Second law of thermodynamics
  C) Third law of thermodynamics
  D) None of the above
- What is the activation energy? (　　)
  A) The energy required for a reaction to occur
  B) The change in concentration of a reactant or product per unit time
  C) The expression that relates the reaction rate to the concentrations of the reac-

tants and the order of the reaction

　　D) The amount of heat required to raise the temperature of a substance by one degree Celsius

- Which of the following is NOT an application of physical chemistry principles? (　　)

　　A) Design and optimization of chemical processes

　　B) Development of new materials

　　C) Understanding and mitigating the environmental impact of chemical processes and materials

　　D) None of the above

- What is the rate law? (　　)

　　A) The energy required for a reaction to occur

　　B) The change in concentration of a reactant or product per unit time

　　C) The expression that relates the reaction rate to the concentrations of the reactants and the order of the reaction

　　D) The amount of heat required to raise the temperature of a substance by one degree Celsius

3.5　Polymer Chemistry

朗读二维码

Polymer chemistry is the branch of chemistry that deals with the study of polymers, which are large molecules composed of repeating subunits called monomers. Polymer chemistry principles are crucial for designing and optimizing polymer-based materials and processes in various industries, such as plastics, adhesives, coatings, and textiles. In this section, we will discuss the basic principles of polymer chemistry and their applications in industry.

(1) Structure and Properties of Polymers

Polymers can have different structures and properties depending on their chemical composition (shown in Figure 3-8), molecular weight, degree of polymerization, and branching.

Some of the properties of polymers that are important for polymer chemistry are listed.

Molecular weight and size distribution: The molecular weight of a polymer determines its physical properties, such as viscosity, solubility, and melting point. The size distribution of polymers affects their mechanical properties, such as stiffness, toughness, and elasticity.

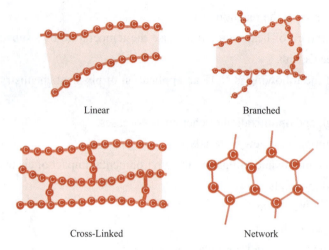

Figure 3-8 Polymer structures

Thermal and mechanical properties: Polymers can have different thermal and mechanical properties depending on their chemical structure and processing conditions. For example, thermoplastics can be molded and shaped by heating and then cooled to set into a desired shape, whereas thermosetting plastics are cured and hardened through irreversible chemical reactions. Chemical and physical properties: Polymers can have different chemical and physical properties depending on their functional groups and intermolecular forces. For example, polar polymers can have good adhesion and wetting properties, while nonpolar polymers can have good barrier and insulation properties.

(2) Polymerization Reactions

Polymerization is the process of forming polymers by connecting monomers through covalent bonds. Polymerization reactions can be classified into two types: addition polymerization and condensation polymerization.

Addition polymerization involves the repeated addition of monomers to a growing polymer chain through a reactive double bond, such as in the polymerization of ethylene to polyethylene.

Condensation polymerization involves the elimination of a small molecule, such as water or alcohol, from two or more monomers to form a polymer chain. An example of this process is the polymerization of nylon from diamine and dicarboxylic acid.

(3) Polymer Characterization

Polymer characterization involves the analysis of the physical and chemical properties of polymers to determine their structure, composition, and performance. Some

of the methods used for polymer characterization are listed below.
- Molecular weight determination: This involves the measurement of the molecular weight and size distribution of polymers by techniques such as gel permeation chromatography (GPC) and light scattering.
- Thermal analysis: This involves the measurement of the thermal properties of polymers by techniques such as differential scanning calorimetry (DSC) and thermogravimetric analysis (TGA).
- Spectroscopic analysis: This involves the measurement of the chemical structure and functional groups of polymers by techniques such as infrared spectroscopy (IR) and nuclear magnetic resonance (NMR).

(4) Applications

Polymer chemistry principles have a wide range of applications in various industries. Some of the applications are:
- Development of new polymer-based materials with specific properties, such as biodegradability, conductivity, and optical transparency;
- Design and optimization of polymer processes for the production of plastics, fibers, films, and composites;
- Characterization of the thermal and mechanical properties of polymers for applications in packaging, automotive, and construction industries;
- Control and optimization of polymer processing conditions, such as temperature, pressure, and additives, for increased yield and quality;
- Understanding and mitigating the environmental impact of polymer processes and materials, such as by recycling and upcycling.

Conclusion

Polymer chemistry principles are essential for designing and optimizing polymer-based materials and processes in various industries. Understanding the structure and properties of polymers, polymerization reactions, and polymer characterization is crucial for anyone working in these industries.

专业词汇

朗读二维码

- polymer chemistry   高分子化学
- subunit   子单元
- monomer   单体
- plastic   塑料
- adhesive   黏合剂
- coating   涂料
- textile   纺织品
- degree of polymerization   聚合度
- size distribution   分子量分布
- stiffness   刚度
- toughness   韧性
- elasticity   弹性
- thermoplastic   热塑性塑料
- thermosetting plastic   热固性塑料
- polar polymer   极性高分子
- nonpolar polymer   非极性高分子
- addition polymerization   加成聚合
- condensation polymerization   缩聚
- nylon   尼龙
- diamine   二胺
- dicarboxylic acid   二羧酸
- gel permeation chromatography (GPC)   凝胶渗透色谱法
- differential scanning calorimetry (DSC)   差示扫描量热法
- thermogravimetric analysis (TGA)   热重分析
- infrared spectroscopy (IR)   红外光谱
- nuclear magnetic resonance (NMR)   核磁共振

常用句型

- Polymer chemistry principles **have a wide range of applications in** various industries. 高分子化学原理在各行各业都有广泛的应用。

  【句型解释】此句型强调某一事物在多个领域中的广泛应用，结构为："某事物 + **have a wide range of applications in** + 各个领域"。表示"在……中有广

3 Basics of Chemistry

泛的应用",用来突出该事物的多功能性和多样化用途。

【例句】Nanotechnology principles **have a wide range of applications in** medicine, electronics, and environmental science. 纳米技术理论在医学、电子学和环境科学中有广泛的应用。

互动练习

- What is polymer chemistry? (   )
    A) The study of metals
    B) The study of large molecules made up of repeating subunits called monomers
    C) The study of acids and bases
    D) The study of organic compounds
- What factors can affect the properties of polymers? (   )
    A) Chemical composition
    B) Molecular weight
    C) Degree of polymerization
    D) All of the above
- What are the two types of polymerization reactions? (   )
    A) Addition and subtraction
    B) Condensation and decomposition
    C) Addition and condensation
    D) Substitution and elimination
- What is the purpose of polymer characterization? (   )
    A) To determine the structure, composition, and performance of polymers
    B) To produce new monomers
    C) To recycle and upcycle polymers
    D) To design and optimize polymer processes
- What are some applications of polymer chemistry? (   )
    A) Development of new polymer-based materials
    B) Characterization of thermal and mechanical properties of polymers
    C) Control and optimization of polymer processing conditions
    D) All of the above

朗读二维码

搜一搜，
检验学习效果

- 化学常用术语的英文测试选择题
- 设计一个无机化学、有机化学、分析化学、物理化学和高分子化学方向的专家一起开会，用英语自我介绍的场景。

Exercises

【Speak & Listen】场景：两位同学正在路上一边走路，一边讨论今天的化学课程。

A: Good morning! How's your chemistry class going today?

B: Oh, it's been quite an adventure! We were discussing the properties of different compounds in organic chemistry. It's like a never-ending puzzle.

A: I know what you mean! Organic chemistry can be quite tricky. I'm still trying to wrap my head around all those functional groups and reactions.

B: Tell me about it! I feel like I need a secret decoder ring just to understand all those complicated chemical structures.

A: Haha, I totally get that! It's like we're detectives trying to decipher(破译) the hidden messages in molecules.

B: Absolutely! And sometimes, it feels like the compounds are playing hide and seek with us. We spend hours trying to track them down in the lab.

A: I can picture it now: a bunch of chemists running around the lab with magnifying glasses(放大镜) and lab coats, shouting "I found you, elusive(难以捉摸的) compound!"

B: Oh, and let's not forget about those moments when a reaction doesn't go as planned. It's like chemistry is playing a prank(恶作剧) on us.

A: Yes, those "Oops" moments when you accidentally mix up the reagents or forget to turn off the Bunsen burner. Chemistry has a mischievous(调皮的) sense of humor sometimes.

B: Definitely! But despite all the challenges and occasional mishaps, chemistry is truly fascinating. It's like a magic show with atoms and molecules as the performers.

A: That's a great way to put it! Chemistry is full of surprises, and we're the lucky audience witnessing the wonders of the molecular world.

B: Absolutely! So, let's keep our lab coats on, our safety goggles strapped, and get ready for more exciting adventures in the world of chemistry!

A: Cheers to that! Here's to our never-ending quest for knowledge and a pinch of humor along the way.

【Write & Read】题目：请写一篇简短的科普文章(100个单词左右)，介绍催化剂在化学反应中的作用及其重要性。

Catalysts: Driving Forces in Chemical Reactions

Catalysts are substances that facilitate chemical reactions by lowering the activation energy required for the reaction to occur. They play a critical role in a wide range of chemical processes and have significant importance in various industries.

Catalysts increase the rate of a reaction without being consumed in the process by providing an alternative reaction pathway with lower energy barriers. This enables reactions to occur under milder conditions and with higher efficiency. Catalysts can be metals, metal oxides, enzymes, or even organic compounds, depending on the specific reaction requirements.

The use of catalysts is vital in many fields, including pharmaceuticals, petrochemicals, and environmental science. They enable the production of important chemicals, such as pharmaceutical drugs, polymers, and clean fuels, while reducing energy consumption and waste generation. Additionally, catalysts are essential in controlling the selectivity and efficiency of chemical reactions, leading to improved product yields and quality.

In conclusion, catalysts are indispensable in chemical reactions as they enhance reaction rates, improve selectivity, and conserve resources. Understanding and developing effective catalysts is fundamental in advancing chemical technologies and achieving sustainable industrial processes.

4

Momentum Transfer Process

搜一搜，
了解专业背景

动量传递原理都讲了些
什么?

流体力学基础都讲了些
什么?

搜一搜，
获取学习资源

流体力学的英文视频
教程

动量传递设备的图片

流体输送设备操作视频

化工流体输送常用术语
的中英文对照

朗读二维码

4.1 Fluid Mechanics Principles

Fluid mechanics is a branch of physics that deals with the study of fluids and their behavior when subjected to different forces. In the chemical and process industries, fluid mechanics principles are crucial for designing and optimizing equipment for the handling, storage, and transportation of fluids. In this section, we will discuss the basic principles of fluid mechanics and their applications in the chemical and process industries.

(1) Fluid Properties

Fluids are substances that can flow and have no fixed shape. They include liquids, gases, and plasmas. The properties of fluids, such as density, viscosity, and surface tension, determine their behavior when subjected to different forces.

Density is the mass per unit volume of a fluid and is expressed in kilograms per cubic meter (kg/m^3). It is an important property in fluid mechanics because it affects the pressure and buoyancy of fluids.

Viscosity is the resistance of a fluid to flow and is expressed in units of pascal seconds (Pa·s) or centipoise (cP). Viscosity is affected by temperature, pressure, and the composition of the fluid.

Surface tension is the property of a fluid that causes it to form a surface film (as depicted in Figure 4-1). It is expressed in units of newtons per meter (N/m) and is affected by the composition of the fluid and the presence of impurities.

(2) Fluid Statics

As shown in Figure 4-2, fluid statics deals with the behavior of fluids at rest or under the influence of static forces. The pressure at a point in a fluid at rest is the same in all directions and is known as hydrostatic pressure. The pressure at a point in a fluid is affected by the fluid's density and depth and is expressed in units of pascal (Pa) or pounds per square inch (psi).

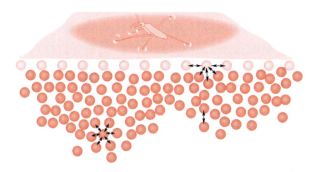

Figure 4-1　Surface tension

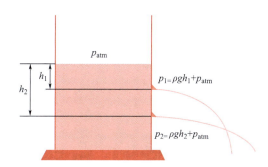

Figure 4-2　Fluid statics

(3) Fluid Dynamics

As depicted in Figure 4-3, fluid dynamics deals with the behavior of fluids in motion. The motion of fluids can be described by the conservation of mass, momentum, and energy.

Mass conservation states that the mass of a fluid is conserved, and any change in the mass of a fluid in a control volume is due to the flow of fluid across its boundaries.

Momentum conservation states that the total momentum of a fluid in a control volume is conserved, and any change in the momentum of a fluid is due to the net force acting on it.

Energy conservation states that the total energy of a fluid in a control volume is conserved, and any change in energy is due to the work done by or on the fluid and the heat transfer.

(4) Applications

Fluid mechanics principles have a wide range of applications in the chemical and process industries. Some of the applications are:

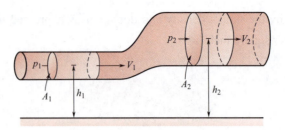

Figure 4-3　Fluid dynamics

- Transportation of fluids through pipelines, such as crude oil, natural gas, and water;
- Design of pumps, compressors, and turbines for fluid transport and energy conversion;
- Mixing and blending of fluids in chemical and food processing;
- Heat transfer in heat exchangers for cooling and heating fluids;
- Fluidized bed reactors for chemical reactions and combustion.

Conclusion

Fluid mechanics principles are essential for designing and optimizing equipment for the handling, storage, and transportation of fluids in the chemical and process industries. Understanding the properties of fluids, fluid statics, and fluid dynamics is crucial for anyone working in these industries. Advances in fluid mechanics continue to improve the efficiency and sustainability of industrial processes.

朗读二维码

专业词汇

- fluid　流体
- viscosity　黏度
- surface tension　表面张力
- fluid statics　流体静力学
- fluid dynamics　流体动力学
- hydrostatic pressure　静水压力
- pascal seconds　帕秒

4 Momentum Transfer Process

- centipoise   厘泊
- mass conservation   质量守恒
- momentum conservation   动量守恒
- energy conservation   能量守恒

常用句型

- Viscosity **is affected by** temperature, pressure, and the composition of the fluid. 黏度受温度、压力和流体成分的影响。

【句型解释】此句型用于描述某一物质或现象受多种因素的影响，结构为："某物质/现象 + **be affected by** + 影响因素"。在这个句型中，**be affected by** 表示"受到……的影响"，是被动语态，强调影响的来源。

【例句】The solubility of a gas in a liquid **is affected by** pressure and temperature. 气体在液体中的溶解度受压力和温度的影响。

互动练习

【英译中】Viscosity is affected by temperature, pressure, and the composition of the fluid. _____
_____

- Which of the following is a fluid? (　　)
  A) Solid
  B) Gas
  C) Plasma
  D) All of the above
- What is viscosity? (　　)
  A) The mass per unit volume of a fluid
  B) The resistance of a fluid to flow
  C) The property of a fluid that causes it to form a surface film
  D) The pressure at a point in a fluid at rest
- What is hydrostatic pressure? (　　)
  A) The pressure at a point in a fluid at rest
  B) The resistance of a fluid to flow
  C) The mass per unit volume of a fluid
  D) The property of a fluid that causes it to form a surface film

- What is momentum conservation? (　　)
  A) The mass of a fluid is conserved
  B) The total momentum of a fluid in a control volume is conserved
  C) The total energy of a fluid in a control volume is conserved
  D) None of the above
- What are some applications of fluid mechanics in the chemical and process industries? (　　)
  A) Transportation of fluids through pipelines
  B) Design of pumps, compressors, and turbines
  C) Mixing and blending of fluids in chemical and food processing
  D) All of the above

4.2 Fluid Transport Equipment

朗读二维码

Fluid conveying equipment, also known as fluid transport equipment, is used to move fluids such as liquids and gases from one place to another in various industries, including chemical, petrochemical, pharmaceutical, and food production. These fluids can be transported through pipelines, pumps, and other equipment. In this section, we will discuss the principles of fluid conveying equipment, their working principles, and applications.

There are several types of fluid conveying equipment used in various industries, including pipelines, pumps, compressors, and valves.

(1) Pipelines

Pipelines are long tubes made of metal, plastic, or composite materials used to transport fluids over long distances (shown in Figure 4-4). Pipelines are an essential component of the oil and gas industry, where they are used to transport crude oil,

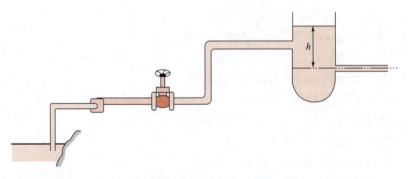

Figure 4-4　Schematic diagram of chemical pipeline system

natural gas, and refined petroleum products. They are also used in the chemical and process industries for the transport of chemicals, water, and wastewater.

(2) Pumps

Pumps are mechanical devices used to move fluids from one place to another. Pumps can be classified into two categories: positive displacement pumps and dynamic pumps. Positive displacement pumps move fluids by trapping a fixed amount of fluid and then forcing it into the discharge pipe, such as reciprocating pump (Figure 4-5) and diaphragm pump (Figure 4-6). Dynamic pumps, on the other hand, move fluids by imparting kinetic energy to the fluid, such as centrifugal pump (Figure 4-7), gear pump (Figure 4-8) and screw pump (Figure 4-9).

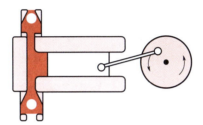

Figure 4-5　Reciprocating pump

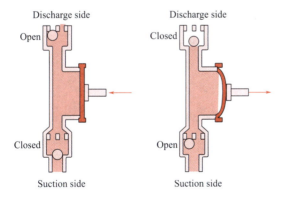

Figure 4-6　Diaphragm pump

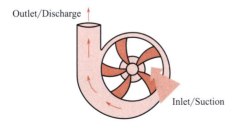

Figure 4-7　Centrifugal pump

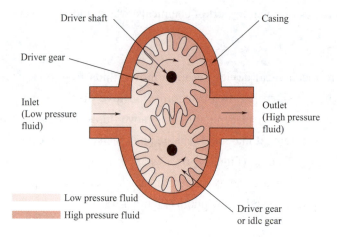

Figure 4-8　Gear pump

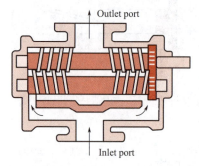

Figure 4-9　Screw pump

（3）Compressors

Compressors are devices used to increase the pressure of gases, such as reciprocating compressor (Figure 4-10), centrifugal blower (Figure 4-11) and roots blower (Figure 4-12). They are used in the oil and gas industry to compress natural gas for transportation through pipelines. Compressors are also used in the chemical industry for the compression of gases used in chemical reactions.

（4）Valves

Valves are devices used to control the flow of fluids through pipes. They can be classified into two categories: stop valves and control valves. Stop valves are used to completely stop the flow of fluid, while control valves are used to regulate the flow of fluid through the pipe. Among them, cut-off valve (Figure 4-13), gate valve (Figure 4-14), and check valve (Figure 4-15) are most commonly used.

4 Momentum Transfer Process

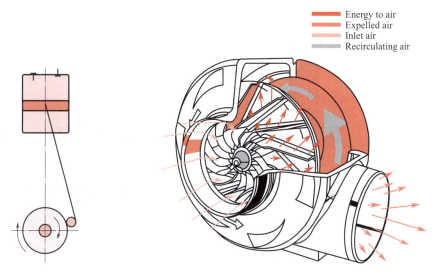

Figure 4-10　Reciprocating compressor

Figure 4-11　Centrifugal blower

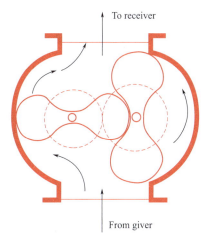

Figure 4-12　Roots blower

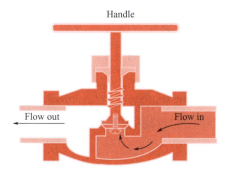

Figure 4-13　Cut-off valve

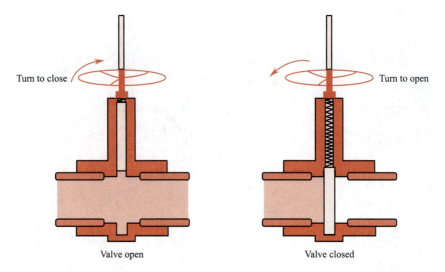

Figure 4-14　Gate valve

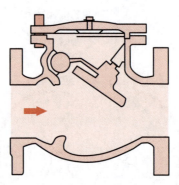

Figure 4-15　Check valve

(5) Applications

Fluid conveying equipment is used in a wide range of industries for the transport of fluids from one place to another. Some of the applications of fluid conveying equipment are:
- Transport of crude oil, natural gas, and refined petroleum products in the oil and gas industry;
- Transport of chemicals in the chemical industry;
- Transport of water and wastewater in the water and wastewater treatment industry;
- Transport of pharmaceutical products in the pharmaceutical industry;
- Transport of food products in the food and beverage industry.

Conclusion

Fluid conveying equipment is an essential component in many industrial processes. Understanding the principles of fluid conveying equipment and the different types available is essential for anyone working in the chemical or process industries. Proper selection, installation, and maintenance of fluid conveying equipment are critical to ensuring the safe and efficient transport of fluids.

专业词汇

朗读二维码

- pipeline system   管线系统
- positive displacement pump   容积式泵
- reciprocating pump   往复泵
- diaphragm pump   隔膜泵
- dynamic pump   动力泵
- gear pump   齿轮泵
- screw pump   螺杆泵
- compressor   压缩机
- reciprocating compressor   往复式压缩机
- centrifugal blower   离心式鼓风机
- roots blower   罗茨鼓风机
- cut-off valve   截止阀
- gate valve   闸阀
- check valve   止回阀

常用句型

- Pipelines **are** long tubes **made of** metal, plastic, or composite materials used to transport fluids over long distances. 管道是由金属、塑料或复合材料制成的长管，用于长距离输送流体。

【句型解释】这句话的典型科技英语句型是"**be made of**",表示由某种材料制成。该句型常用于描述物品或设备的材质。

【例句】The valve **is made of** brass. 这个阀门是由黄铜制成的。

- Dynamic pumps, **on the other hand**, move fluids by imparting kinetic energy to the fluid.

【句型解释】这句话的典型科技英语句型是"**on the other hand**",表示与之前提到的事物相对比。该句型常用于在描述两个相反的事物时使用。

【例句】Positive displacement pumps move fluids by trapping a fixed amount of fluid, **on the other hand**, dynamic pumps move fluids by imparting kinetic energy to the fluid. 正位移泵通过截留一定量的流体来输送流体,而动力泵则通过向流体传递动能来输送流体。

互动练习

【英译中】The pump is made of stainless steel. _____

【中译英】截止阀完全停止流体的流动,而控制阀则通过管道调节流体的流动。_____

- What is the main function of fluid conveying equipment? (   )
  A) To create fluids
  B) To store fluids
  C) To move fluids from one place to another
  D) To measure fluids
- What are the four types of fluid conveying equipment? (   )
  A) Pipelines, pumps, compressors, and turbines
  B) Pipes, valves, tanks, and reactors
  C) Pumps, compressors, mixers, and agitators
  D) Pipelines, pumps, compressors, and valves
- What is the difference between positive displacement pumps and dynamic pumps? (   )
  A) Positive displacement pumps move fluids by imparting kinetic energy to the fluid, while dynamic pumps move fluids by trapping a fixed amount of fluid and then forcing it into the discharge pipe
  B) Positive displacement pumps move fluids by trapping a fixed amount of fluid and then forcing it into the discharge pipe, while dynamic pumps move fluids by imparting kinetic energy to the fluid

C) Positive displacement pumps and dynamic pumps are the same

D) Positive displacement pumps and dynamic pumps are not used in fluid conveying equipment

- What are the two categories of valves? (   )

  A) Positive valves and negative valves

  B) Stop valves and control valves

  C) Dynamic valves and static valves

  D) Gas valves and liquid valves

- In which industries is fluid conveying equipment commonly used? (   )

  A) Chemical industry only

  B) Petrochemical industry only

  C) Pharmaceutical industry only

  D) Various industries including chemical, petrochemical, pharmaceutical, and food production

4.3 Non-Homogeneous Separation Equipment

朗读二维码

Heterogeneous mixtures, which consist of two or more phases with different physical and chemical properties, are frequently encountered in the chemical and process industries. The separation of these phases is a critical step in many industrial processes, such as oil and gas production, chemical production, and wastewater treatment. Non-homogeneous separation equipment is used to separate these mixtures into their constituent phases. In this section, we will discuss the principles of non-homogeneous separation equipment, their working principles, and applications.

There are several types of non-homogeneous separation equipment used in the chemical and process industries. These include sedimentation, filtration, centrifugation, and extraction.

(1) Sedimentation

Sedimentation is the process of separating solid particles from a liquid or gas mixture by allowing the particles to settle under the influence of gravity. The separation is based on the differences in the densities of the phases. As Figure 4-16 depicted, the solid particles settle to the bottom of the container, while the liquid or gas phase remains at the top. The efficiency of the sedimentation process depends on factors such as particle size, particle density, and fluid viscosity.

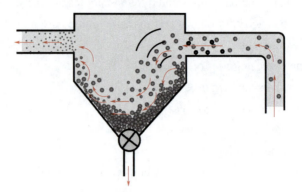

Figure 4-16　Gravitational settler

(2) Filtration

Filtration is the process of separating solid particles from a liquid or gas mixture by passing the mixture through a porous medium. The porous medium retains the solid particles, while the liquid or gas phase passes through. Filtration is used for the removal of solid particles from liquids or gases, and the efficiency of the process depends on factors such as the size of the pores in the filter medium, the pressure applied to the mixture, and the properties of the particles and the fluid. Figure 4-17 and Figure 4-18 show the commonly used filters in the chemical industry.

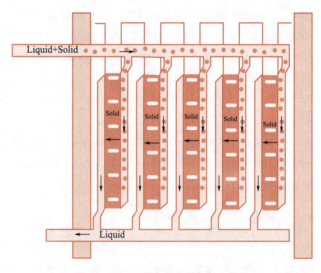

Figure 4-17　Plate and frame filter

(3) Centrifugation

Centrifugation is the process of separating the components of a heterogeneous mixture by applying centrifugal force as shown in Figure 4-19 and Figure 4-20.

4 Momentum Transfer Process

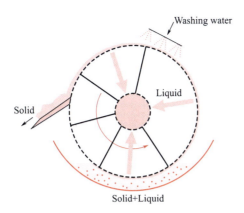

Figure 4-18　Rotary drum vacuum filter

The mixture is placed in a rotating container, and the centrifugal force separates the components based on their density and size. The heavier components move towards the outer edge of the container, while the lighter components remain towards the center. Centrifugation is commonly used for the separation of suspensions, emulsions, and immiscible liquids.

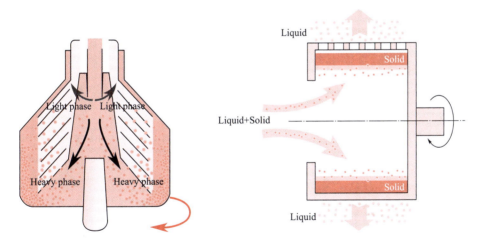

Figure 4-19　Centrifugal settler　　　Figure 4-20　Centrifugal filter

(4) Extraction

Extraction is the process of separating a solute from a solvent by using a second solvent. As depicted in Figure 4-21, the solute is dissolved in the second solvent, and the two solvents are then separated by using non-homogeneous separation equipment such as decanters, centrifuges, or filters. Extraction is used for the separation of organic compounds, such as oils and fats, from aqueous solutions.

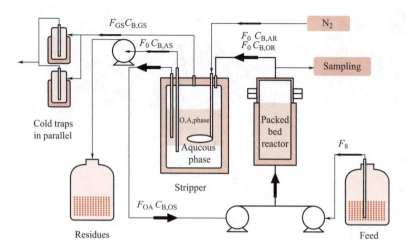

Figure 4-21   Extractor

(5) Applications

Non-homogeneous separation equipment is used in a wide range of industries, such as chemical production, food and beverage production, pharmaceuticals, and wastewater treatment. Some of the applications of non-homogeneous separation equipment are:

- Separation of suspended solids from wastewater in municipal and industrial treatment plants;
- Separation of oil and water in the oil and gas industry;
- Separation of protein from whey in the dairy industry;
- Separation of blood components in the medical industry;
- Separation of catalysts and reaction products in the chemical industry.

Conclusion

Non-homogeneous separation equipment is an essential component in many industrial processes. Understanding the principles of non-homogeneous separation equipment and the different types available is essential for anyone working in the chemical or process industries.

4 Momentum Transfer Process

专业词汇

- heterogeneous mixtures　不均匀混合物
- sedimentation　沉淀
- gravitational settler　重力沉降器
- porous medium　多孔介质
- decanters　分离器
- plate and frame filter　板框过滤机
- rotary drum vacuum filter　旋转真空过滤机
- centrifugal force　离心力
- centrifugal settler　离心沉降器
- centrifugal filter　离心过滤器
- immiscible liquids　不相溶液体
- extractor　萃取器

朗读二维码

常用句型

- The efficiency of the sedimentation process **depends on** factors such as particle size, particle density, and fluid viscosity. 沉积过程的效率取决于颗粒大小、颗粒密度和流体黏度等因素。

【句型解释】该句型为"X **depends on** factors such as Y, Z, and W.", 表示 X 的效率或结果取决于因素 Y、Z 和 W 等多个因素的综合影响。其中, Y、Z 和 W 是具体的因素名称。

【例句】The extraction yield **depends on** factors such as the choice of solvents, extraction time, and temperature. 萃取收率取决于溶剂的选择、萃取时间和温度等因素。

互动练习

【英译中】The filtration efficiency depends on factors such as the size of the pores, pressure applied, and properties of the particles and fluid._____
_____

- What is sedimentation? (　　)
  A) The process of separating solid particles from a liquid or gas mixture by

passing the mixture through a porous medium

B) The process of separating a solute from a solvent by using a second solvent

C) The process of separating solid particles from a liquid or gas mixture by allowing the particles to settle under the influence of gravity

D) The process of separating the components of a heterogeneous mixture by applying centrifugal force

- What is the purpose of filtration? (   )

  A) To separate the components of a heterogeneous mixture by applying centrifugal force

  B) To separate a solute from a solvent by using a second solvent

  C) To separate solid particles from a liquid or gas mixture by allowing the particles to settle under the influence of gravity

  D) To separate solid particles from a liquid or gas mixture by passing the mixture through a porous medium

- Which non-homogeneous separation equipment is used for the separation of organic compounds, such as oils and fats, from aqueous solutions? (   )

  A) Sedimentation

  B) Filtration

  C) Centrifugation

  D) Extraction

- What are some applications of non-homogeneous separation equipment? (   )

  A) Separation of oil and water in the oil and gas industry

  B) Separation of protein from whey in the dairy industry

  C) Separation of suspended solids from wastewater in municipal and industrial treatment plants

  D) All of the above

- What is the efficiency of the sedimentation process dependent on? (   )

  A) Particle size, particle density, and fluid viscosity

  B) Size of the pores in the filter medium, the pressure applied to the mixture, and the properties of the particles and the fluid

  C) Density and size of the components of the mixture

  D) The solubility of the solute in the second solvent

对话音频

搜一搜,
检验学习效果

- 化工流体输送过程与设备常用术语的英文测试选择题

- 设计一个围绕泵、压缩机和阀门作用的英文讨论

Exercises

【Speak & Listen】场景：两位学生正在咖啡店讨论期末考试。

B: Hey, do you remember the formula for momentum transfer?

A: Umm, let me think... Oh, I got it! It's rho times A times V, right?

B: Nope, that's the formula for mass transfer. Momentum transfer is rho times

A times *V* squared.

A: Oh no, I always get those confused. Thanks for correcting me, Bob.

B: No problem. Speaking of momentum transfer, have you heard about the new energy drink that's popular among chemical engineers?

A: No, I haven't. What's it called?

B: It's called "Momentum Maximizer" and it claims to transfer momentum from the drink to the person who consumes it.

A: Wow, that sounds impressive. Does it really work?

B: I don't know, but I heard that some students tried it and they ended up running around the campus like crazy.

A: Haha, I don't think I'll try it then. I don't want to end up causing a momentum transfer accident.

B: Good idea. Let's stick to coffee for now. It may not give us momentum, but at least it won't make us run around like headless chickens.

A: Agreed. Now let's get back to studying momentum transfer before our exam turns into a momentum disaster.

B: Sounds like a plan. Let's maximize our momentum and ace this exam!

A: (laughs) You always know how to make studying fun.

【Write & Read】写一小段作文 (100 个单词左右), 解释动量传递的概念及其在化学工程中的重要性。

Momentum Transfer in Chemical Engineering

Momentum transfer is a crucial concept in chemical engineering, used in the design and operation of fluid handling systems. Momentum transfer is the transfer of momentum from one fluid to another or from a fluid to a solid surface. Chemical engineers rely on momentum transfer to understand and predict fluid behavior and to design and optimize fluid handling systems for maximum efficiency.

There are two types of momentum transfer: convective momentum transfer and diffusive momentum transfer. Convective momentum transfer involves the transfer of momentum due to the movement of fluid, while diffusive momentum transfer involves the transfer of momentum due to the diffusion of momentum from areas of high concentration to areas of low concentration.

Understanding momentum transfer is essential for chemical engineers as it allows them to design and optimize fluid handling systems for efficient and safe operation.

5

Heat Transfer Process

朗读二维码

搜一搜，
了解专业背景

热传递的三种形式
有哪些？

热交换器的种类有
哪些？

搜一搜，
获取学习资源

热传递过程视频
热交换器运作原理
换热器的图片
蒸发器的图片
干燥器的图片
结晶器的图片
化工传热过程常用术语
的中英文对照

5.1 Principles and Processes of Heat Transfer

Heat transfer is a fundamental process in chemical engineering and plays a critical role in many industrial processes. It involves the exchange of thermal energy between two or more systems with different temperatures. Understanding heat transfer principles and processes is crucial for designing and optimizing various heat transfer equipment, including heat exchangers, reactors, and furnaces. In this section, we will discuss the principles of heat transfer, the different modes of heat transfer, and their applications.

(1) Principles of Heat Transfer

Heat transfer is governed by the fundamental laws of thermodynamics. The first law of thermodynamics, also known as the law of conservation of energy, states that energy cannot be created or destroyed but can only be transferred from one form to another. The second law of thermodynamics states that heat always flows from hotter to cooler objects and that the efficiency of a heat transfer process is limited by the Carnot efficiency.

As shown in Figure 5-1, heat transfer can occur through three modes: conduction, convection, and radiation.

(2) Conduction

Conduction is the transfer of heat through a medium without the movement of the medium itself. Heat transfer occurs due to the collisions of molecules in the medium. The rate of heat transfer by conduction is dependent on the thermal conductivity of the medium, the thickness of the medium, and the temperature difference between the two systems.

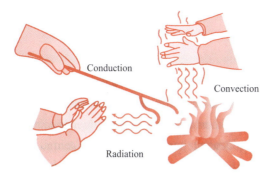

Figure 5-1　Heat transfer modes

(3) Convection

Convection is the transfer of heat through the movement of a fluid. Heat transfer occurs due to the bulk movement of the fluid, which results in the mixing of hot and cold fluids. Convection can occur through natural convection, where the fluid movement is caused by buoyancy forces, or through forced convection, where an external force, such as a pump, is used to move the fluid.

(4) Radiation

Radiation is the transfer of heat through electromagnetic waves. Radiation can occur in vacuum and does not require a medium for heat transfer. The rate of heat transfer by radiation is dependent on the temperature of the emitting body, the temperature of the receiving body, and the distance between the two bodies.

(5) Applications

Heat transfer is a critical process in many industrial applications, including the following aspects.

- Heat exchangers: Heat exchangers are used for the transfer of heat between two fluids, often in different phases, to either heat or cool a process stream. Heat exchangers are used in industries such as chemical production, power generation, and refrigeration.
- Reactors: Heat transfer plays a significant role in the design and operation of chemical reactors. The understanding of heat transfer mechanisms is essential in optimizing reaction conditions, improving reactor performance, and minimizing the risk of thermal runaway.
- Furnaces: Furnaces are used in various industries, such as steel production and glass manufacturing, for high-temperature processes. The understanding of heat transfer mechanisms is essential in designing and optimizing furnace operation, improving energy efficiency, and reducing emissions.

Conclusion

Heat transfer is a fundamental process in chemical engineering and plays a critical role in many industrial processes. Understanding heat transfer principles and processes and their applications is essential for anyone working in the chemical or process industries. The development of new heat transfer technologies and the improvement of existing ones are crucial for improving process efficiency, reducing energy consumption, and minimizing the environmental impact of industrial processes.

朗读二维码

专业词汇

- thermal energy　热能
- exchange　交换
- modes　模式
- conduction　传导
- convection　对流
- radiation　辐射
- electromagnetic waves　电磁波
- thermal conductivity　热导率
- thermal runaway　热失控
- energy efficiency　能效
- environmental impact　环境影响

常用句型

- The rate of heat transfer by conduction **is dependent on** the thermal conductivity of the medium, the thickness of the medium, and the temperature difference between the two systems. 传导传热的速率取决于介质的导热系数、介质的厚度以及两个系统之间的温差。
【句型解释】本句采用了"主语+动词+介词短语"结构，其中介词短语为"**dependent on**",表示"取决于",常用于科技文献中,表达某个因素对另一个因素的影响。

【例句】The efficiency of a solar cell **is dependent on** the material used in its construction. 太阳能电池的效率取决于其建造时所使用的材料。

- The understanding of heat transfer mechanisms **is essential in optimizing** reaction conditions, **improving** reactor performance, **and minimizing** the risk of thermal runaway. 了解传热机制对于优化反应条件、提高反应器性能和最大限度地降低热失控风险至关重要。

【句型解释】本句采用了"名词性从句＋动词＋宾语＋并列连接词＋动词＋宾语＋并列连接词＋动词＋宾语"结构,其中并列连接词为"and",表示"和",用于连接三个并列动词短语。该句型常用于科技文献中,表达某个概念或思想对某个方面的重要性或影响。

【例句】The understanding of genetic mutations is essential in diagnosing diseases, developing treatments, and improving patient outcomes. 了解基因突变对于诊断疾病、开发治疗方法和提高治疗效果至关重要。

互动练习

【英译中】The quality of the product is dependent on the precision of the manufacturing process._____
_____

【中译英】开发新材料对于提高太阳能电池的效率、降低成本和提高耐用性至关重要。_____
_____

- What is the first law of thermodynamics?(   )
    A) Energy cannot be created or destroyed but can only be transferred from one form to another
    B) Heat always flows from hotter to cooler objects
    C) The rate of heat transfer by radiation is dependent on the temperature of the emitting body, the temperature of the receiving body, and the distance between the two bodies
    D) The efficiency of a heat transfer process is limited by the Carnot efficiency
- What is convection?(   )
    A) The transfer of heat through electromagnetic waves
    B) The transfer of heat through the movement of a fluid
    C) The transfer of heat through a medium without the movement of the medium

itself

D) None of the above

- What is the role of heat transfer in reactor design? (   )

    A) Improving reactor performance

    B) Minimizing the risk of thermal runaway

    C) Optimizing reaction conditions

    D) All of the above

- What is the purpose of heat exchangers? (   )

    A) To transfer heat between two fluids, often in different phases, to either heat or cool a process stream

    B) To improve reactor performance

    C) To design and optimize furnace operation

    D) None of the above

- What is radiation? (   )

    A) The transfer of heat through electromagnetic waves

    B) The transfer of heat through the movement of a fluid

    C) The transfer of heat through a medium without the movement of the medium itself

    D) None of the above

5.2 Heat Transfer Equipment

朗读二维码

Heat transfer is an important process in many industrial applications, such as chemical production, power generation, and food processing. Heat transfer equipment is used to transfer heat from one medium to another, such as from a hot fluid to a cold fluid. In this section, we will discuss the principles of heat transfer equipment, their working principles, and applications.

There are several types of heat transfer equipment used in the chemical and process industries. These include heat exchangers, boilers, condensers, evaporators, and heaters.

(1) Heat Exchangers

As shown in Figure 5-2, a heat exchanger is a device used to transfer heat between two fluids. The fluids can either be in direct contact or they can be separated by a solid wall. Heat exchangers are classified based on their construction, such as shell and tube, plate and frame, and spiral. The efficiency of a heat exchanger depends on factors such as the flow rate of the fluids, the temperature difference between the fluids, and the heat transfer coefficient of the fluids.

5 Heat Transfer Process

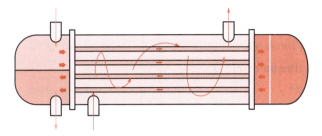

Figure 5-2　Heat exchanger

(2) Boilers

A boiler is a device used to generate steam or hot water by heating a fluid as depicted in Figure 5-3. The fluid can be water, steam, or a mixture of both. Boilers are classified based on their construction, such as fire tube, water tube, and electric. The efficiency of a boiler depends on factors such as the heat transfer surface area, the fuel type, and the combustion efficiency.

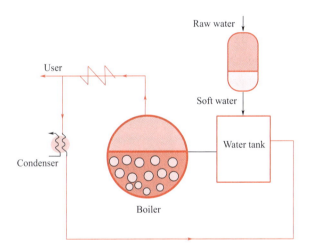

Figure 5-3　Water cycle in the boiler house

(3) Condensers

A condenser is a device used to condense a vapor into a liquid by removing heat. The vapor can be steam, refrigerant, or any other volatile substance. Condensers are classified based on their construction, such as surface, jet, and surface-jet. The efficiency of a condenser depends on factors such as the cooling medium, the vapor pressure, and the heat transfer coefficient.

(4) Evaporators

An evaporator is a device used to vaporize a liquid by removing heat. The liquid can be water, solvents, or any other volatile substance. Evaporators are classified based on their construction, such as falling film, rising film, and forced circulation. The efficiency of an evaporator depends on factors such as the heat transfer surface area, the flow rate of the liquid, and the evaporation rate.

(5) Heaters

A heater is a device used to heat a fluid or gas. The fluid or gas can be air, water, oil, or any other substance. Heaters are classified based on their construction, such as tubular, cartridge, and immersion. The efficiency of a heater depends on factors such as the heat transfer surface area, the power input, and the temperature difference between the fluid and the heater.

(6) Applications

Heat transfer equipment is used in a wide range of industries, such as chemical production, food and beverage production, pharmaceuticals, and power generation. Some of the applications of heat transfer equipment are:

- Heating or cooling of process fluids in chemical production;
- Cooling of liquids in the food and beverage industry;
- Boiling water to produce steam for power generation;
- Heating or cooling of gases in Heating Ventilation and Air Conditioning (HVAC) systems.

Conclusion

Heat transfer equipment is a crucial part of many industrial processes. Understanding the principles of heat transfer equipment and the different types available is essential for anyone working in the chemical or process industries.

专业词汇

- heat exchanger 换热器
- boiler 蒸汽发生器
- condenser 冷凝器

5 Heat Transfer Process

- evaporator　蒸发器
- heater　加热器
- tubular　管式
- cartridge　夹套式
- immersion　沉浸式
- falling film　降膜
- rising film　升膜
- forced circulation　强制循环
- HVAC(Heating Ventilation and Air Conditioning) systems　供暖通风与空气调节系统

常用句型

- The efficiency of a heat exchanger depends on **factors such as** the flow rate of the fluids, the temperature difference between the fluids, and the heat transfer coefficient of the fluids. 热交换器的效率取决于流体的流速、流体之间的温差以及流体的传热系数等因素。

【句型解释】该句型为复合句，其中主句为"The efficiency of a heat exchanger depends on **factors**"，从句为"**such as** the flow rate of the fluids, the temperature difference between the fluids, and the heat transfer coefficient of the fluids"，用于具体说明主句中的"factors"。从句中采用了"such as"的结构，用于列举具体的因素。

【例句】The performance of a wind turbine depends on **factors such as** wind speed, air density, and blade design. 风力涡轮机的性能取决于风速、空气密度和叶片设计等因素。

互动练习

【英译中】Such as shell and tube heat exchangers, plate heat exchangers are commonly used in the chemical industry._____

【中译英】换热器中可以使用不同种类的传热介质，如水、蒸汽和热油等。

- What isheat exchanger? (　　)

  A) A device used to transfer heat between two fluids

  B) A device used to generate steam or hot water by heating a fluid

  C) A device used to condense a vapor into a liquid by removing heat

  D) A device used to vaporize a liquid by removing heat

- Which of the following is NOT a type of heat transfer equipment? (　　)

  A) Heat exchanger

  B) Boiler

  C) Cooling tower

  D) Evaporator

- What is a boiler used for? (　　)

  A) To transfer heat between two fluids

  B) To condense a vapor into a liquid by removing heat

  C) To vaporize a liquid by removing heat

  D) To generate steam or hot water by heating a fluid

- What factors affect the efficiency of a condenser? (　　)

  A) The flow rate of the fluids, the temperature difference between the fluids, and the heat transfer coefficient of the fluids

  B) The heat transfer surface area, the fuel type, and the combustion efficiency

  C) The cooling medium, the vapor pressure, and the heat transfer coefficient

  D) The heat transfer surface area, the flow rate of the liquid, and the evaporation rate

- What is the application of heat transfer equipment in the food and beverage industry? (　　)

  A) Heating or cooling of process fluids in chemical production

  B) Boiling water to produce steam for power generation

  C) Cooling of liquids in the food and beverage industry

  D) Heating or cooling of gases in HVAC systems

对话音频

搜一搜，检验学习效果

- 化工传热过程与设备常用术语的英文测试选择题
- 设计一个围绕三种不同传热形式的英文对话

Exercises

【Speak & Listen】场景：两位学生 A 和 B，他们正在图书馆准备传热课程的期末考试。

A: Do you remember the different modes of heat transfer?

B: Yeah, there's conduction, convection, and radiation. But why are we even studying this? I thought we were going to be designing chemical processes, not building ovens.

A: (laughs) Well, heat transfer is an important part of chemical engineering. If we can't transfer heat efficiently, our processes won't work properly.

B: I guess you're right. So, how do you remember the different heat transfer methods?

A: I have a trick. I always think of it as cooking. Conduction is like using a pan on a stove, convection is like using an oven, and radiation is like using a microwave.

B: (laughs) That's a funny way to remember it. But speaking of cooking, have you tried that new ramen place near campus? They use a heat transfer method that's out of this world!

A: Really? What kind of method?

B: They use infrared radiation to cook the noodles! It's super-fast and the noodles come out perfectly every time.

A: Wow, that's amazing. I guess we can apply heat transfer engineering to cooking as well.

B: Yeah, and if we ever get tired of designing chemical processes, we can always open our own restaurant!

A: (laughs) That's a good backup plan. But let's focus on our exam for now. We don't want to fail and end up cooking ramen for a living.

B: Agreed. Let's transfer some heat from our brains to our pencils and ace this exam!

A: (laughs) You always know how to make studying fun.

【Write & Read】写一小段作文 (100 个单词左右),解释传热的概念及其在化学工程中的重要性。

Heat Transfer in Chemical Engineering

Heat transfer is a fundamental concept in chemical engineering, involved in the design and operation of processes that involve the transfer of heat. Heat transfer is the exchange of thermal energy between objects or systems. Chemical engineers rely on efficient heat transfer to ensure that chemical processes operate at the desired temperature, maximizing process efficiency.

There are three types of heat transfer: conduction, convection, and radiation. Conduction is the transfer of heat between two materials in contact. Convection is the transfer of heat through the movement of fluids. Radiation is the transfer of heat through electromagnetic waves.

Understanding heat transfer is essential for chemical engineers, allowing them to design and optimize processes to operate at the correct temperature, with minimal energy loss, and maximum efficiency.

6

Mass Transfer Process

搜一搜，
了解专业背景

化工质量传递过程
有哪些？

化工分离设备都有
哪些？

什么叫精馏？

搜一搜，
获取学习资源

化工质量传递视频

化工分离设备图片

化工分离过程与设备常
用术语的中英文对照

6.1　Principles of Mass Transfer

Mass transfer is an essential process in chemical engineering that involves the movement of components from one phase to another. Mass transfer equipment is used to facilitate this transfer in a wide range of industrial processes. Here, we will discuss the principles of mass transfer processes and the factors that affect them.

(1) Principles of Mass Transfer Processes

Mass transfer processes occur due to a concentration difference between two phases. The driving force for mass transfer is the concentration gradient, which is defined as the difference in concentration between the two phases. The rate of mass transfer is proportional to the concentration gradient, the interfacial area between the two phases, and the mass transfer coefficient.

There are several types of mass transfer processes, including diffusion (Figure 6-1), convection, and dispersion. Diffusion is the movement of molecules or ions from a high concentration to a low concentration region. Convection is the movement of mass due to bulk fluid flow. Dispersion is the mixing of two or more substances due to random motion.

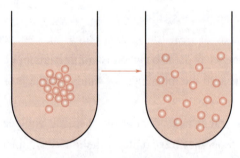

Figure 6-1　Diffusion

(2) Factors Affecting Mass Transfer

Several factors affect mass transfer processes. The most important factors are listed below.

- Concentration difference: The concentration difference between two phases is the driving force for mass transfer.
- Temperature: Temperature affects the rate of mass transfer by changing the viscosity of the fluid and the diffusion coefficient of the components.
- Pressure: Pressure affects the solubility of the components and the interfacial tension between the two phases.
- Interfacial area: The interfacial area between the two phases affects the rate of mass transfer. Increasing the interfacial area can increase the rate of mass transfer.
- Mass transfer coefficient: The mass transfer coefficient depends on the physical properties of the components, the type of mass transfer, and the equipment used.

(3) Applications

Mass transfer equipment is used in a wide range of industrial processes.

- Distillation: Distillation is used for the separation of two or more components based on their boiling points.
- Absorption: Absorption is used for the removal of a component from a gas stream by dissolving it in a liquid.
- Membrane separation: Membrane separation is used for the separation of components based on their molecular size or charge.

Conclusion

Mass transfer is an essential process in chemical engineering, and mass transfer equipment is used in a wide range of industrial processes. Understanding the principles of mass transfer and the factors that affect it is essential for anyone working in the chemical or process industries. By using the appropriate mass transfer equipment and optimizing the process conditions, it is possible to achieve efficient and cost-effective mass transfer operations.

Part 2 Specialized English for Chemistry and Chemical Engineering

专业词汇

- mass transfer　质量传递
- concentration gradient　浓度梯度
- interfacial area　界面面积
- mass transfer coefficient　质量传递系数
- diffusion　扩散
- diffusion coefficient　扩散系数
- solubility　溶解度
- bulk fluid flow　主体流体流动
- dispersion　分散
- random motion　随机运动
- dissolving　溶解
- distillation　精馏
- absorption　吸收
- membrane separation　膜分离

常用句型

- The rate of mass transfer is **proportional to** the concentration gradient, the interfacial area between the two phases, and the mass transfer coefficient. 传质速率与浓度梯度、两相界面面积和传质系数成正比。

  【句型解释】这句话使用了"**be proportional to**"的结构，表示两个量之间的关系是成比例的。在这个句型中，"the rate of mass transfer"和"the concentration gradient、the interfacial area、the mass transfer coefficient"之间有一定的数学关系，即前者与后者之间的关系是成比例的。

  【例句】The amount of oxygen diffused through the membrane **is proportional to** the surface area of the membrane and the concentration gradient across the membrane. 在膜扩散过程中，氧气的扩散量与膜的表面积和跨膜浓度梯度成正比。

- Membrane separation is used for the separation of components **based on** their molecular size or charge. 膜分离可用来分离成分根据其分子大小或电荷。

  【句型解释】这句话使用了"**based on**"的结构，表示某种行为或结果是基于某个特定的因素或条件。在这个句型中，"the separation of components"与"their molecular size or charge"之间的关系是基于前者对后者的依赖或影响。

6 Mass Transfer Process

【例句】The design of the reactor is **based on** the reaction kinetics and the desired conversion. 反应釜的设计是基于反应动力学和所需转化率。

互动练习

【英译中】The rate of heat transfer is proportional to the temperature difference and the thermal conductivity of the material. _____
_____

【中译英】萃取过程中溶剂的选择是基于目标化合物在该溶剂中的溶解度。
_____
_____

- What is the driving force for mass transfer? (   )
  A) Interfacial area
  B) Temperature
  C) Pressure
  D) Concentration gradient
- Which type of mass transfer process involves the movement of mass due to bulk fluid flow? (   )
  A) Diffusion
  B) Convection
  C) Dispersion
  D) None of the above
- Which of the following factors does NOT affect the rate of mass transfer? (   )
  A) Concentration difference
  B) Temperature
  C) Pressure
  D) Viscosity of the fluid
- What is distillation used for? (   )
  A) Separation of components based on their boiling points
  B) Removal of a component from a gas stream by dissolving it in a liquid
  C) Separation of a component from a mixture using a solvent
  D) Separation of components based on their molecular size or charge
- What is membrane separation used for? (   )
  A) Separation of components based on their boiling points
  B) Removal of a component from a gas stream by dissolving it in a liquid
  C) Separation of a component from a mixture using a solvent
  D) Separation of components based on their molecular size or charge

6.2 Mass Transfer Equipment

Mass transfer equipment is an essential component in many industrial processes, especially those involving the separation or transfer of different components from a mixture. The separation of components from a mixture is crucial in various industries such as chemical production, pharmaceuticals, food and beverage production, and wastewater treatment. Here, we will discuss the principles of mass transfer equipment, their working principles, and applications. There are several types of mass transfer equipment used in chemical and process industries. These include distillation, absorption, adsorption, and membrane separation.

(1) Distillation

Distillation is the process of separating different components of a mixture by heating it to a specific temperature to vaporize one or more components, which are then condensed and collected separately, as shown in Figure 6-2. The separation relies on the differences in the boiling points of the components. Distillation is used for the separation of different components from liquids or gases, and the efficiency of the process depends on factors such as the boiling points of the components and the pressure applied to the mixture.

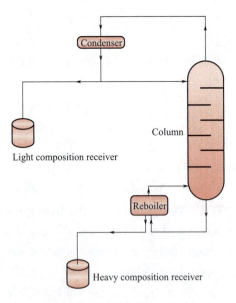

Figure 6-2 Distillation column

(2) Absorption

Absorption is the process of separating a gas component from a gas mixture by dissolving the gas component in a liquid solvent. As shown in Figure 6-3, the gas mixture is brought into contact with the solvent, and the gas component is absorbed into the liquid phase. Absorption is used for the removal of impurities, such as carbon dioxide, from gas streams.

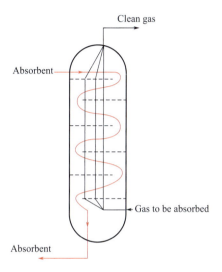

Figure 6-3　Absorption tower

(3) Adsorption

As shown in Figure 6-4, adsorption is the process of separating a gas or liquid component from a mixture by adhering it to a solid surface. The solid surface is called the adsorbent, and the component that is adhered to the surface is called the adsorbate. Adsorption is used for the separation of different components from gases or liquids, such as the removal of impurities from natural gas.

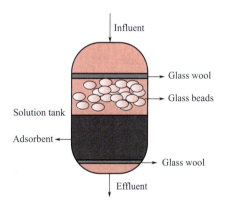

Figure 6-4　Adsorption tower

(4) Membrane Separation

Membrane separation is the process of separating different components from a mixture by using a membrane, which is a thin layer of material that allows only certain components to pass through it. As shown in Figure 6-5, the separation is based on the size and chemical properties of the components. Membrane separation is used for the separation of different components from liquids or gases, such as the removal of salt from seawater.

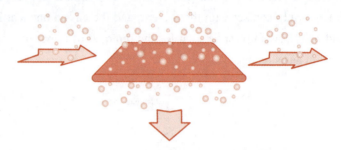

Figure 6-5　Membrane separation process

(5) Applications

Mass transfer equipment is used in a wide range of industries, such as chemical production, food and beverage production, pharmaceuticals, and wastewater treatment. Some of the applications of mass transfer equipment are:

- Separation of ethanol from water in the production of alcoholic beverages;
- Removal of carbon dioxide from natural gas in the gas processing industry;
- Separation of essential oils from plants in the production of perfumes and flavors;
- Removal of impurities from crude oil in the petroleum industry;
- Purification of water in the production of drinking water.

Conclusion

Mass transfer equipment is an essential component in many industrial processes. Understanding the principles of mass transfer equipment and the different types available is essential for anyone working in the chemical or process industries. The selection of the appropriate mass transfer equipment depends on the specific application, the physical and chemical properties of the mixture, and the desired outcome.

6 Mass Transfer Process

专业词汇

朗读二维码

- distillation column　精馏塔
- condense　冷凝，凝结
- distillation column(tower)　精馏塔
- absorption column(tower)　吸收塔
- adsorption column(tower)　吸附塔
- adhere　黏附，附着
- adsorbent　吸附剂
- adsorbate　吸附物
- aqueous　水的，水溶液的

常用句型

- The separation **relies on** the differences in the boiling points of the components.
（蒸馏）分离的依据是各成分沸点的不同。

【句型解释】在本文中，该句型用来解释蒸馏的分离原理，即不同组分的沸点差异。此句型用于描述某个过程或现象的基础、原理或机制，结构为："主语 + **rely on** + 短语"。

【例句】The extraction process **relies on** the solubility of the solute in the second solvent. 提取过程依赖于溶质在第二种溶剂中的溶解度。

互动练习

【英译中】The separation relies on the affinity of the gas component for the liquid solvent._____
_____

- What is the process of distillation used for? (　　)
  A) Separation of gases from liquids
  B) Separation of liquids from solids
  C) Separation of different components from liquids or gases
  D) Separation of solids from gases

95

- What is absorption? (　　)

  A) Separation of a gas component from a gas mixture by dissolving the gas component in a liquid solvent

  B) Separation of different components from gases or liquids by adhering them to a solid surface

  C) Separation of a solute from a solvent by using a second solvent

  D) Separation of different components from a mixture by using a membrane

- What is adsorption? (　　)

  A) Separation of a gas or liquid component from a mixture by adhering it to a solid surface

  B) Separation of different components from gases or liquids by adhering them to a solid surface

  C) Separation of a solute from a solvent by using a second solvent

  D) Separation of different components from a mixture by using a membrane

- What is the process of extraction used for? (　　)

  A) Separation of gases from liquids

  B) Separation of liquids from solids

  C) Separation of different components from liquids or gases

  D) Separation of a solute from a solvent by using a second solvent

- What is membrane separation? (　　)

  A) Separation of a gas or liquid component from a mixture by adhering it to a solid surface

  B) Separation of different components from gases or liquids by using a membrane

  C) Separation of a solute from a solvent by using a second solvent

  D) Separation of different components from liquids or gases by dissolving the gas component in a liquid solvent.

Exercises

【Speak & Listen】场景：两位学生正在咖啡馆准备传质分离课程的期末考试。

A: Hey, do you remember the different types of mass transfer?

B: Yeah, there's diffusion, convection, and dispersion. But to be honest, I'm having a hard time remembering which is which.

A: I know what you mean. I always get them mixed up too. But don't worry, we'll figure it out before the exam.

B: Speaking of mass transfer, have you seen the new smoothie shop on campus?

搜一搜，
检验学习效果

- 化工分离过程与设备常用术语的英文测试选择题
- 设计一个化工分离过程的英文对话训练

A: No, I haven't. What's so special about it?

B: They use a mass transfer method that's supposed to make their smoothies extra smooth.

A: Really? What kind of method?

B: They use a homogenizer to break down the fruit fibers into smaller particles, which makes the smoothies smoother.

A: (laughs) I guess we can apply mass transfer engineering to food as well.

B: Yeah, who knew that making a smoothie could be so complicated? But at least we'll be able to explain the science behind it to our friends.

A: (laughs) Yeah, we'll be the smoothie experts on campus. But let's focus on our exam for now. We don't want to fail and end up making smoothies for a living.

B: Agreed. Let's transfer some knowledge from our notes to our brains and ace this exam!

A: (laughs) You always know how to make studying fun.

【Write & Read】写一小段作文 (100 个单词左右)，解释传质的概念及其在分离过程中的重要性.

Mass Transfer in Separation Processes

Mass transfer is an essential concept in separation processes, enabling the separation of different components or substances in a mixture. Mass transfer refers to the movement of a component or substance from one phase to another, such as from a liquid to a gas or from a solid to a liquid.

Separation processes, such as distillation, absorption, extraction, and membrane separation, rely on mass transfer to achieve separation. Distillation separates components based on differences in volatility, absorption separates a gas from a mixture by absorbing it into a liquid, extraction uses a solvent to extract a solute from a liquid mixture, and membrane separation separates components based on differences in size or chemical properties.

By understanding mass transfer, engineers can design efficient separation processes used in various applications, such as the production of fuels, chemicals, and pharmaceuticals. Mass transfer is a critical concept in separation processes, enabling the efficient separation of different components in a mixture.

7

Chemical Reaction Process

朗读二维码

搜一搜，
了解专业背景

化学反应动力学讲的
什么？

化工反应设备有哪些
种类？

搜一搜，
获取学习资源

化学反应设备的视频

生成带有搅拌器、换热器、轴封和釜体的化学反应釜的图片

化学反应设备运行动画

化学反应过程常用术语的中英文对照

7.1 Chemical Reaction Kinetics Principles

Chemical reactions are at the heart of the chemical and process industries, where they are used to produce a wide range of products, from fuels and plastics to pharmaceuticals and fertilizers. The study of chemical reaction kinetics, which deals with the rates and mechanisms of chemical reactions, is essential for the design, optimization, and control of chemical processes. In this section, we will discuss the principles of chemical reaction kinetics, including reaction rates, rate laws, and reaction mechanisms.

（1）Reaction Rate

The reaction rate is defined as the change in the concentration of a reactant or product per unit time. It is usually expressed in terms of moles per liter per second [mol/(L·s)]) or in other suitable units. The reaction rate depends on several factors, including the concentrations of the reactants, the temperature, the pressure, the surface area of the reactants, and the presence of catalysts or inhibitors.

（2）Rate Law

The rate law is an equation that relates the reaction rate to the concentrations of the reactants and other factors. The rate law is determined experimentally by measuring the reaction rate at different concentrations of the reactants and fitting the data to an equation. The rate law can be used to predict the effect of changing the concentrations of the reactants or other factors on the reaction rate.

（3）Reaction Mechanism

The reaction mechanism is the sequence of elementary steps that occur during a chemical reaction. It describes how the reactants are transformed into the products and the intermediates that are formed along the way. The reaction mechanism is usually inferred from experimental data, such as the rate law, the reaction order, and the activation energy.

(4) Catalysis

Catalysis is the process of increasing the rate of a chemical reaction by the addition of a substance called a catalyst, as shown in Figure 7-1. Catalysts work by providing an alternative reaction pathway with a lower activation energy. The catalyst lowers the activation energy of the reaction, which makes it easier for the reactants to form the products. Catalysts are used in many industrial processes to increase the efficiency and selectivity of the reactions.

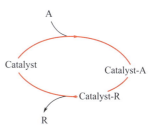

Figure 7-1　Catalysis cycle

(5) Applications

The principles of chemical reaction kinetics are used in a wide range of industries, such as chemical production, petrochemicals, pharmaceuticals, and materials science. Some of the applications of chemical reaction kinetics are:
- Design and optimization of chemical reactors;
- Production of fuels and chemicals from biomass;
- Development of new pharmaceuticals and materials;
- Understanding the environmental impact of chemical reactions;
- Control and monitoring of industrial processes.

Conclusion

Chemical reaction kinetics is an essential component in the design and optimization of chemical processes. Understanding the principles of the reaction rate, the rate law, and the reaction mechanism is essential for anyone working in the chemical or process industries. The application of these principles to industrial processes can lead to more efficient and sustainable production of chemicals, fuels, and materials.

专业词汇

- chemical reaction kinetics 化学反应动力学
- reaction rate 反应速率
- rate law 速率方程
- inhibitor 抑制剂
- elementary step 基元反应
- reaction order 反应级数
- activation energy 活化能
- selectivity 选择性
- petrochemicals 石油化工
- biomass 生物质
- conversion rate 转化率

常用句型

- The reaction mechanism **is usually inferred from** experimental data, such as the rate law, the reaction order, and the activation energy. 反应机理通常是根据实验数据推断出来的，如速率方程、反应级数和活化能。

【句型解释】该句型中，主语是"The reaction mechanism"，谓语动词是"**inferred**"，宾语是"**from** experimental data"。从该句中可以看出，该句型是一个复杂句，其中包含了一个从句 (such as the rate law, the reaction order, and the activation energy)。该句型用来表达化学反应机理是如何推断出来的，需要通过实验数据 (如速率方程、反应级数、活化能等) 来进行推断。

【例句】Scientists can **infer** the reaction mechanism **from** the analysis of the reaction order and other experimental data. 科学家们可以通过分析反应级数和其他实验数据来推断反应机理。

- Catalysts work **by providing** an alternative reaction pathway with a lower activation energy. 催化剂的作用是提供活化能较低的替代反应途径。

【句型解释】这个句型是一个复合句，其中包含主语"Catalysts"、谓语"work"和一个由介词短语"**by providing** an alternative reaction pathway with a lower activation energy"引导的由动词"providing"构成的现在分词短语作方式状语。

【例句】Catalysts can increase the rate of a chemical reaction **by providing** an alternative reaction pathway with a lower activation energy. 催化剂可以通过提供

7 Chemical Reaction Process

一活化能更低的替代反应路径来提高化学反应的速率。

互动练习

【英译中】The reaction mechanism of this reaction is inferred from the experimental data obtained from the rate law and activation energy measurements. _____
_____

【中译英】催化剂的效果取决于其提供具有更低活化能的替代反应路径的能力。反应器的选择取决于反应特征。_____
_____

- What is the definition of reaction rate? (   )
    A) The sequence of elementary steps that occur during a chemical reaction
    B) The change in the concentration of a reactant or product per unit time
    C) The equation that relates the reaction rate to the concentrations of the reactants
    D) The process of increasing the rate of a chemical reaction by the addition of a substance called a catalyst

- What is the rate law? (   )
    A) The sequence of elementary steps that occur during a chemical reaction
    B) The change in the concentration of a reactant or product per unit time
    C) The equation that relates the reaction rate to the concentrations of the reactants
    D) The process of increasing the rate of a chemical reaction by the addition of a substance called a catalyst

- What is the reaction mechanism? (   )
    A) The sequence of elementary steps that occur during a chemical reaction
    B) The change in the concentration of a reactant or product per unit time
    C) The equation that relates the reaction rate to the concentrations of the reactants
    D) The process of increasing the rate of a chemical reaction by the addition of a substance called a catalyst

- What is the purpose of a catalyst in a chemical reaction? (   )
    A) To change the concentrations of the reactants
    B) To change the temperature of the reaction
    C) To increase the efficiency and selectivity of the reaction
    D) To increase the pressure of the reaction

- What are some applications of chemical reaction kinetics? (　　)
    A) Understanding the principles of the reaction rate, the rate law, and the reaction mechanism
    B) Design and optimization of chemical reactors
    C) Production of fuels and chemicals from biomass
    D) All of the above

7.2　Chemical Reaction Processes

Chemical reaction processes can be classified into three types: homogeneous reactions, gas-solid reactions, and gas-liquid reactions. Homogeneous reactions occur when all the reactants are in the same phase, either liquid or gas. Gas-solid reactions occur when a gas reacts with a solid, while gas-liquid reactions occur when a gas reacts with a liquid. Understanding the different types of chemical reaction processes is important for designing and optimizing chemical processes in various industries.

(1) Homogeneous Reaction Processes

Homogeneous reactions are chemical reactions that occur in a single phase, either a liquid or a gas. In these reactions, the reactants and products are uniformly mixed, and the reaction rate is typically determined by the concentration of the reactants. Homogeneous reactions are widely used in the chemical industry, including the production of chemicals, pharmaceuticals, and fuels.

The rate law for homogeneous reactions can be determined experimentally by measuring the change in concentration of the reactants over time. The rate law is typically expressed as a mathematical equation that relates the rate of the reaction to the concentrations of the reactants, temperature, and other factors. For example, the rate law for the reaction A + B ⟶ C might be expressed as:

$$\text{Rate} = k\, c_A^m\, c_B^n$$

where k is the rate constant; m and n are the reaction orders with respect to A and B, respectively; c_A and c_B are the concentrations of A and B, respectively.

(2) Gas-Solid Reaction Processes

Gas-solid reactions occur when a gas reacts with a solid (Figure 7-2). These reactions are widely used in metallurgy, combustion, and catalysis. In these reactions, the rate is typically determined by the surface area of the solid, which determines the number of active sites available for the reaction.

The rate law for gas-solid reactions can be expressed as:

$$\text{Rate} = kS(p - p^*)$$

where k is the rate constant; S is the surface area of the solid; p is the pressure of the gas; and p^* is the equilibrium pressure of the gas at the surface of the solid. This equation is known as the Langmuir equation.

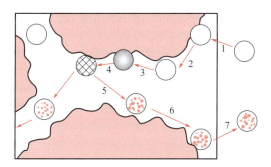

Figure 7-2 Gas-solid reaction processes steps
1- external diffusion, 2- internal diffusion, 3- adsorption, 4- interfacial reaction,
5- desorption, 6- internal diffusion, 7- external diffusion

(3) Gas-Liquid Reaction Processes

Gas-liquid reactions occur when a gas reacts with a liquid. These reactions are widely used in the chemical and petroleum industries. In these reactions, the rate is typically determined by the mass transfer of the gas into the liquid, which is influenced by factors such as the surface area of the liquid, the solubility of the gas in the liquid, and the diffusion coefficient of the gas in the liquid.

The rate law for gas-liquid reactions can be expressed as:

$$\text{Rate} = kLa(c^* - c)$$

where k is the rate constant; L is the interfacial area between the gas and liquid phases; a is the mass transfer coefficient; c^* is the equilibrium concentration of the gas in the liquid; and c is the actual concentration of the gas in the liquid. This equation is known as the Hatta number equation.

Conclusion

The knowledge of homogeneous, gas-solid, and gas-liquid reactions is crucial for the production of chemicals, pharmaceuticals, and fuels in the chemical industry. Understanding the reaction process is essential for increasing the efficiency and selectivity of chemical reactions, which has a significant impact on the sustainability and profitability of industrial processes.

朗读二维码

专业词汇

- activation energy   活化能
- equilibrium pressure   平衡压力
- interfacial area   界面面积
- Langmuir equation   朗缪尔方程式
- Hatta number equation   八田数方程式
- active sites   活性位点
- selectivity   选择性
- homogeneous catalysts   均相催化剂
- heterogeneous catalysts   异相催化剂

常用句型

- **The knowledge of** homogeneous, gas-solid, and gas-liquid reactions is crucial for the production of chemicals, pharmaceuticals, and fuels in the chemical industry. 均相反应、气-固反应和气-液反应的知识对于化学工业中化学品、药品和燃料的生产至关重要。

    【句型解释】这个句型包含主语"**The knowledge of** homogeneous, gas-solid, and gas-liquid reactions"、谓语"is crucial for"和一个由介词短语"for the production of chemicals, pharmaceuticals, and fuels in the chemical industry"引导的作用状语。

    【例句】**The knowledge of** homogeneous, gas-solid, and gas-liquid reactions is

7 Chemical Reaction Process

fundamental to the design and optimization of chemical reactors. 均相反应、气-固反应和气-液反应理论对于化学反应器的设计和优化至关重要。

互动练习

【英译中】Understanding the principles of homogeneous, gas-solid, and gas-liquid reactions is essential for developing new chemical processes._____
_____

- Which of the following reactions would be considered a homogeneous reaction? ( )
  A) $H_2\ (g) + O_2\ (g) \longrightarrow H_2O_2\ (l)$
  B) $CO\ (g) + H_2O\ (g) \longrightarrow CO_2\ (g) + H_2\ (g)$
  C) $2Na\ (s) + Cl_2\ (g) \longrightarrow 2NaCl\ (s)$
  D) $HCl\ (aq) + NaOH\ (aq) \longrightarrow NaCl\ (aq) + H_2O\ (l)$
- Which of the following reactions would be considered a gas-solid reaction? ( )
  A) $2Na\ (s) + Cl_2\ (g) \longrightarrow 2NaCl\ (s)$
  B) $2H_2\ (g) + O_2\ (g) \longrightarrow 2H_2O\ (g)$
  C) $Fe\ (s) + 2HCl\ (g) \longrightarrow FeCl_2\ (s) + H_2\ (g)$
  D) $N_2\ (g) + 3H_2\ (g) \longrightarrow 2NH_3\ (g)$
- Which of the following equations represents the rate law for a homogeneous reaction? ( )
  A) Rate = $kS(p - p^*)$
  B) Rate = $kLa(c^* - c)$
  C) Rate = $kc_A^m c_B^n$
  D) Rate = k
- Which of the following equations represents the rate law for a gas-liquid reaction? ( )
  A) Rate = $kS(p - p^*)$
  B) Rate = $kLa(c^* - c)$
  C) Rate = $kc_A^m c_B^n$
  D) Rate = k
- Which of the following statements about catalysts is true? ( )
  A) Catalysts are consumed in the reaction
  B) Catalysts provide an alternative reaction pathway with a higher activation energy
  C) Catalysts increase the efficiency and selectivity of reactions

D) Catalysts have no effect on the rate of a reaction

7.3 Chemical Reaction Equipment

Chemical reaction equipment is an essential component of the chemical industry, where it is used to transform raw materials into products through chemical reactions. The design and operation of chemical reaction equipment are critical factors in achieving high yields, selectivity, and efficiency in chemical processes. In this section, we will discuss the principles of chemical reaction equipment, including reactor types, reactor design, and reactor operation.

(1) Reactor Types

As Figure 7-3, Figure 7-4, Figure 7-5 and Figure 7-6 showed, there are several types of chemical reactors, including batch reactors, continuous stirred-tank reactors (CSTRs), plug-flow reactors (PFRs), fixed-bed reactors, fluidized-bed reactors and various types of gas-liquid reactors.

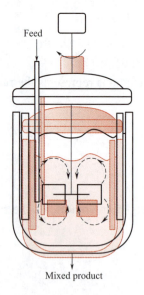

Figure 7-3　Tank reactor

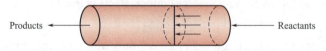

Figure 7-4　Plug-flow reactor

7 Chemical Reaction Process

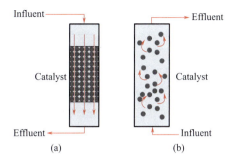

Figure 7-5 Fixed-bed reactor(a) and fluidized-bed reactor(b)

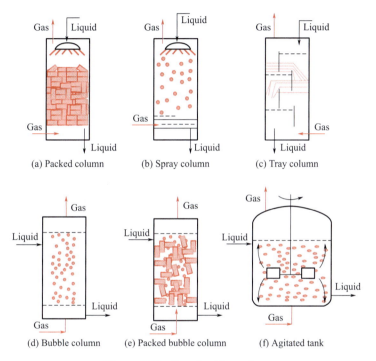

Figure 7-6 Gas-liquid reactors

Each reactor type has its advantages and disadvantages, depending on the specific applications. Batch reactors [Figure 7-7(a)] are the simplest and most versatile type of reactor, but they have limited productivity and are not suitable for continuous processes. CSTRs [Figure 7-7(d), (e)] are commonly used in large-scale chemical processes due to their ability to operate continuously and maintain uniform reaction conditions. Semi-continuous reactors [Figure 7-7(b), (c)], offer a compromise between batch and continuous processes, allowing for more controlled and efficient operations in certain applications.

PFRs (Figure 7-4) are well-suited for highly exothermic reactions and can achieve high conversion rates, but they are difficult to operate and control. FBRs [Figure 7-5(a)] are used for reactions involving solid particles and have high mass

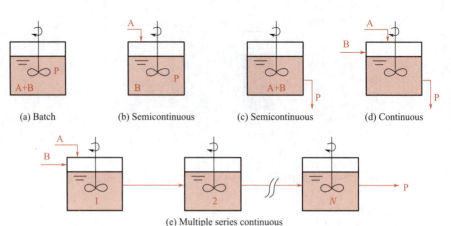

Figure 7-7 Operation types of chemical tank reactors

and heat transfer rates, but they require careful control of fluidization conditions.

(2) Reactor Design

The design of chemical reactors is based on the reaction kinetics, thermodynamics, and transport phenomena involved in the process. The key design parameters include the reactor size, shape, and configuration, as well as the heat and mass transfer rates. The reactor design should ensure that the reaction proceeds at the desired rate while maintaining safe operating conditions. The design should also consider the material of construction, as well as corrosion, erosion, and fouling effects.

(3) Reactor Operation

The operation of chemical reactors is critical in achieving high yields, selectivity, and efficiency in chemical processes. The operating conditions, such as temperature, pressure, and flow rate, should be controlled to maintain optimal reaction conditions. The choice of operating conditions depends on the specific reaction kinetics and thermodynamics. In addition, the choice of catalyst and the use of additives, such as inhibitors or promoters, can also affect the reactor operation.

(4) Applications

The principles of chemical reaction equipment are used in a wide range of industries, such as chemical production, petrochemicals, pharmaceuticals, and materials science. Some of the applications of chemical reaction equipment are:
- Production of bulk chemicals, such as fertilizers, plastics, and polymers;
- Production of specialty chemicals, such as pharmaceuticals, agrochemicals, and fine chemicals;
- Production of fuels, such as gasoline, diesel, and jet fuel;

- Treatment of wastewater and air pollutants;
- Production of renewable energy, such as biofuels and hydrogen.

Conclusion

Chemical reaction equipment is an essential component in the chemical industry, where it is used to transform raw materials into products through chemical reactions. The design and operation of chemical reactors are critical factors in achieving high yields, selectivity, and efficiency in chemical processes. Understanding the principles of reactor types, reactor design, and reactor operation is essential for anyone working in the chemical or process industries. The applications of these principles to industrial processes can lead to more efficient and sustainable productions of chemicals, fuels, and materials.

专业词汇

朗读二维码

- batch reactor (BR)　间歇搅拌釜式反应器
- continuous stirred-tank reactor (CSTR)　连续搅拌釜式反应器
- plug-flow reactor (PFR)　活塞流反应器，平推流反应器
- fixed-bed reactor　固定床反应器
- fluidized-bed reactor　流化床反应器
- packed column reactor　填料塔反应器
- spray column reactor　喷淋塔反应器
- tray column reactor　板式塔反应器
- bubble column reactor　鼓泡塔反应器
- packed bubble column reactor　填料鼓泡塔反应器
- agitated bubble column reactor　搅拌鼓泡塔反应器
- erosion　侵蚀
- fouling effects　污垢效应

常用句型

- The reactor design **should ensure that** the reaction proceeds at the desired rate while maintaining safe operating conditions. 反应器的设计应确保反应以理想的速度进行，同时保持安全的操作条件。

【句型解释】该句型为"**should ensure that**"结构，表示应该确保某种情况发生。该结构常用于科技英语中的建议、要求、规定等表达中。

【例句】The software **should ensure that** the data is securely encrypted during transmission. 软件应确保数据在传输过程中得到安全加密。

互动练习

【英译中】The design of the reactor should ensure that it can withstand high temperature and pressure._____

- What is the advantage of continuous stirred-tank reactors (CSTRs)? (　　)
  A) They are simple and versatile
  B) They have high conversion rates
  C) They are suitable for continuous processes
  D) They are well-suited for exothermic reactions
- Which reactor type is well-suited for highly exothermic reactions? (　　)
  A) Batch reactors
  B) Continuous stirred-tank reactors (CSTRs)
  C) Plug-flow reactors (PFRs)
  D) Fluidized-bed reactors (FBRs)
- What are the key design parameters for chemical reactors? (　　)
  A) The operating conditions, such as temperature, pressure, and flow rate
  B) The reactor material of construction
  C) The size, shape, and configuration of the reactor
  D) The choice of catalyst and the use of additives
- What are some applications of chemical reaction equipment? (　　)
  A) Production of bulk chemicals and fuels
  B) Treatment of wastewater and air pollutants
  C) Production of renewable energy
  D) All of the above

- Why is understanding the principles of chemical reaction equipment important?
  ( )
  A) It can lead to more efficient and sustainable production of chemicals, fuels, and materials
  B) It is necessary to work in the chemical or process industries
  C) It is important for safety reasons
  D) It is required for regulatory compliance

Exercises

【Speak & Listen】场景：两位学生正在咖啡馆准备传质分离课程的期末考试。

对话音频

搜一搜，
检验学习效果

- 化工反应过程与设备常用术语的英文测试选择题
- 设计化学反应设备旁的工程师与操作员的简单英文对话

B: Hey, do you remember the different types of chemical reactions?

A: Yeah, there's synthesis, decomposition, combustion, and so on. But to be honest, I'm having a hard time keeping track of them all.

B: I know what you mean. There are so many reactions to remember. But don't worry, we'll figure it out before the exam.

A: Speaking of chemical reactions, have you heard about the new energy drink that's supposed to give you superpowers?

B: (laughs) What are you talking about?

A: It's called "Super Reaction" and it claims to enhance your reaction time and cognitive abilities.

B: (laughs) That's ridiculous. There's no chemical reaction that can give you superpowers.

A: I know, I know. But it's still interesting to think about the chemical reactions that are happening in our bodies when we drink something like that.

B: Yeah, it is. And that's why we're studying chemical reaction engineering, to understand the science behind reactions like that.

A: (laughs) I guess we'll have to use our knowledge for good instead of trying to become superheroes.

B: Agreed. Let's transfer some knowledge from our notes to our brains and ace this exam!

A: (laughs) You always know how to make studying fun.

【Write & Read】写一小段作文(100个单词左右),描述化学反应器安全的重要性。

Safety in Chemical Reactors

Safety is paramount in chemical reactors due to the potential hazards associated with chemical reactions.

Chemical reactions can produce a significant amount of heat, leading to a rise in temperature and pressure that can result in an explosion or a runaway reaction.

Additionally, chemicals used in reactions can be toxic, flammable, or corrosive, causing harm to workers and the environment. Therefore, it is crucial to prioritize safety measures in the design, equipment, and procedures of chemical reactors.

Proper ventilation, emergency shut-off systems, and personal protective equipment should be in place to protect workers and prevent accidents. Regular maintenance and inspections should be conducted to ensure the reactor is in good condition and operating safely.

By prioritizing safety, we can ensure that chemical reactions are carried out in a safe and responsible manner, preventing accidents and minimizing harm to workers and the environment.

Part 3

Practical English for Chemical Engineering

化工行业呈现出高端化、多样化、集成化的趋势，其从业人员的岗位也越来越面向品种多样的新产品开发以及来自高度集成化的大型企业，因此能够熟练使用实验室开发以及化工大型生产现场的常用英语变得格外重要。

让学生在未来的职业实践中，更好地用英语进行工作上的沟通，是本部分内容的设置目的。

8

Chemical Laboratory Practical English

朗读二维码

搜一搜，
了解专业背景

化学实验室的实验设备
化学实验室的常用操作

搜一搜，
获取学习资源

化学实验室操作视频
化学实验室安全注意事项视频
化学实验室操作常用术语的中英文对照

8.1 Laboratory Apparatus and Operation

Chemistry experimental apparatus refers to the equipment, tools, and materials used in chemical experiments to collect data and conduct measurements. The selection of experimental apparatus depends on the specific experiment being conducted, the chemicals being used, and the level of precision required.

Figure 8-1, Figure 8-2 and Figure 8-3 are some common examples of chemistry experimental apparatus.

Beaker　　　　　　　Erlenmeyer flask　　　　　Flat-bottomed flask

Round-bottomed flask　　　　Three necked flask

Figure 8-1　Commonly used glassware

8 Chemical Laboratory Practical English

Hot plate

Heating mantle

Oil bath

Hot air tool

Figure 8-2　Commonly used heating apparatus

Top-loading balance

Analytical balance

Measuring cylinder

Figure 8-3　Commonly used measurement tools

Other usually used equipment in laboratory including thermometer, stirrer, filter paper, funnel, reflux condenser and separatory funnel. There are many modern chemical analysis instruments available today.

- Mass spectrometry (MS): a technique that ionizes molecules and measures their mass-to-charge ratio. MS can be used to identify and quantify compounds in complex mixtures.
- Nuclear magnetic resonance (NMR) spectroscopy: a technique that uses magnetic fields and radio waves to determine the structure and composition of molecules.
- X-ray diffraction (XRD): a technique that uses X-rays to determine the crystal structure of materials.
- Gas chromatography (GC): a technique that separates and analyzes the components of a mixture based on their volatility.
- High-performance liquid chromatography (HPLC): a technique that separates and analyzes the components of a mixture based on their chemical and physical properties.
- Infrared (IR) spectroscopy: a technique that uses infrared radiation to identify and characterize chemical compounds.
- UV-Visible (UV-Vis) spectroscopy: a technique that uses ultraviolet and visible light to measure the absorption or transmission of light by a sample.

Conclusion

Chemistry experimental apparatus is essential in conducting chemical experiments, and the selection and use of the proper equipment can greatly impact the accuracy and reliability of the results obtained. There are many other types of instruments and techniques available, each with its own strengths and limitations. The choice of instrument depends on the specific application and the type of sample being analyzed.

朗读二维码

专业词汇

- glassware 玻璃器皿
- beaker 烧杯

8 Chemical Laboratory Practical English

- Erlenmeyer flask   锥形瓶
- flat-bottomed flask   平底烧瓶
- round-bottomed flask   圆底烧瓶
- three necked flask   三口烧瓶
- heating apparatus   加热装置
- hot plate   加热板
- heating mantle   加热套
- oil bath   油浴
- hot air tool   热风枪
- measurement tool   称量工具
- top-loading balance   上皿式天平
- analytical balance   分析天平
- measuring cylinder   量筒
- thermometer   温度计
- stirrer   搅拌器
- filter paper   滤纸
- funnel   漏斗
- reflux condenser   回流冷凝器
- separatory funnel   分液漏斗
- mass spectrometry   质谱法
- nuclear magnetic resonance   核磁共振
- X-ray diffraction   X射线衍射
- Gas chromatography (GC)   气相色谱
- High-performance liquid chromatography (HPLC)   高效液相色谱
- Infrared (IR) spectroscopy   红外光谱
- UV-Visible (UV-Vis) spectroscopy   紫外可见光谱

常用句型

- There are many other types of instruments and techniques available, **each with its own strengths and limitations**. 还有许多其他类型的仪器和技术，每种都有自己的优势和局限性。
- 【句型解释】"**each with its own strengths** (advantages) **and limitations** (disadvantages)"，该句型可以用于表明几种情况各有千秋。
　　【例句】Various types of spectrometers are used in chemical analysis, **each with its own advantages and limitations**. 化学分析时用到多种类型的光谱仪，每种都有自己的优势和局限性。

Part 3 Practical English for Chemical Engineering

互动练习

- What is the purpose of chemistry experimental apparatus? (　　)
  A) To collect data and conduct measurements
  B) To analyze data and interpret results
  C) To develop new chemical theories
  D) To generate hypotheses for future experiments
- What factors influence the selection of experimental apparatus? (　　)
  A) The level of precision required
  B) The chemicals being used
  C) The specific experiment being conducted
  D) All of the above
- Which technique can be used to identify and quantify compounds in complex mixtures? (　　)
  A) Nuclear magnetic resonance (NMR) spectroscopy
  B) X-ray diffraction (XRD)
  C) Gas chromatography (GC)
  D) Infrared (IR) spectroscopy
- What is the purpose of UV-Visible (UV-Vis) spectroscopy? (　　)
  A) To identify and characterize chemical compounds using infrared radiation
  B) To measure the absorption or transmission of light by a sample using ultraviolet and visible light
  C) To determine the crystal structure of materials using X-rays
  D) To separate and analyze the components of a mixture based on their chemical and physical properties
- What is the purpose of high-performance liquid chromatography (HPLC)? (　　)
  A) To identify and quantify compounds in complex mixtures
  B) To determine the crystal structure of materials
  C) To separate and analyze the components of a mixture based on their volatility
  D) To separate and analyze the components of a mixture based on their chemical and physical properties

8.2 Commonly Used Conversation in Chemical Laboratory

Here are some examples of commonly used conversations that might occur in a chemical laboratory.

- Requesting a chemical: "Can you pass me the hydrochloric acid, please?"
- Confirming safety procedures: "Did you put on your safety goggles before starting the experiment?"
- Clarifying instructions: "Can you repeat that step? I didn't quite catch it."
- Reporting observations: "The solution turned blue after adding the indicator."
- Discussing results: "The concentration of the solution was measured to be 0.25 mol/L."
- Asking for assistance: "I'm having trouble calibrating the pH meter. Can you help me?"
- Giving instructions: Make sure to heat the mixture to 80℃ for 10 minutes."
- Confirming equipment availability: "Is the spectrophotometer available for use right now?"
- Discussing safety concerns: "I noticed a spill on the floor. We should clean it up to prevent any accidents."
- Giving feedback: "Good job on completing the experiment. Let's review the results together."

These are just a few examples, and the conversations that occur in a chemical laboratory may vary depending on the specific experiment being conducted and the individuals involved. However, communication is essential in a laboratory to ensure safety, accuracy, and successful completion of experiments.

专业词汇

- goggle　护目镜
- confirming safety procedures　确认安全程序
- clarifying instructions　弄清指示
- reporting observations　报告观察结果
- discussing results　讨论结果

Part 3 Practical English for Chemical Engineering

- asking for assistance　请求帮助
- giving instructions　给出指示
- confirming equipment availability　确认设备可用性
- discussing safety concerns　讨论安全问题
- spectrophotometer　分光光度计
- spill　泄漏
- giving feedback　给予反馈

常用句型

- **Make sure to heat** the mixture to 80℃ for 10 minutes. 确保将混合物加热至 80℃ 10 分钟。

  【句型解释】命令句型"**make sure to do**"和"**make sure that**"用于表达指示或命令某个操作步骤，强调需要确保的事项。虽然两者意思相近，但在句子结构上有所不同。**make sure to do** 用于强调做某事前某个具体的操作步骤必须被执行；**make sure that** 用于强调做某事前确保某个情况或条件必须得到满足。

  【例句1】**Make sure to calibrate** the equipment before use. 确保在使用前校准设备。

  【例句2】Before starting the experiment, **make sure that** all safety measures are in place. 在进行实验前，确保所有的安全措施都已经准备好了。

互动练习

【英译中】Make sure that all files are saved before you shut down the computer.
_____
_____

【中译英】确保在处理化学品之前戴上防护手套。_____

- What is the importance of communication in a chemical laboratory? (　　)
  A) To ensure safety, accuracy, and successful completion of experiments
  B) To request chemicals
  C) To confirm equipment availability
  D) To give feedback
- Which conversation is an example of requesting assistance? (　　)

A) "Can you pass me the hydrochloric acid, please?"

B) "Did you put on your safety goggles before starting the experiment?"

C) "I'm having trouble calibrating the pH meter. Can you help me?"

D) "Make sure to heat the mixture to 80 ℃ for 10 minutes."

- What is the importance of confirming safety procedures in a chemical laboratory? (   )

  A) To prevent accidents and ensure personal safety

  B) To clarify instructions

  C) To report observations

  D) To discuss results

- Which conversation is an example of discussing safety concerns? (   )

  A) "The solution turned blue after adding the indicator."

  B) "I'm having trouble calibrating the pH meter. Can you help me?"

  C) "I noticed a spill on the floor. We should clean it up to prevent any accidents."

  D) "Good job on completing the experiment. Let's review the results together."

- What is the importance of giving feedback in a chemical laboratory? (   )

  A) To improve future experiments and results

  B) To request chemicals

  C) To clarify instructions

  D) To discuss safety concerns

Exercises

- 【Speak & Listen】实验室里的对话

  ### 场景1：化学实验室中

  A: Hey, do you know how to use this equipment?

  B: Uh, I'm not really sure. Have you read the manual?

  A: Yeah, but it's all in English. I wish we had a manual in emoji.

  B: Haha, that would make things a lot easier. Maybe we can use the fire emoji to indicate when things get too hot to handle.

  A: And the poop emoji to indicate when we make a mistake?

  B: Uh, maybe we should stick to the traditional labeling system for that.

  ### 场景2：测量实验中

  A: This ruler doesn't have any units on it.

  B: Yeah, I think it's a metric ruler.

  A: Well, I don't speak metric. Can you translate for me?

  B: Sure, it's pretty simple. 10 millimeters is equal to one centimeter, and 100 centimeters is equal to one meter.

对话音频

搜一搜，
检验学习效果

- 设计一个发生在化学实验室里的简单英文对话
- 设计一个实验室安全操作的英文讨论训练

A: Okay, I think I got it. But how many football fields is that?

B: Uh, I don't think that's a standard unit of measurement in science.

场景3：化学实验室中

A: Do you have any idea what these chemicals smell like?

B: Hmm, let me take a whiff.

A: Be careful, it could be toxic.

B: (coughing) Whoa, that smells like my ex's perfume.

A: Uh, I don't think that's a helpful reference point.

B: Sorry, I just can't help but notice the similarity.

场景4：质量控制实验中

A: Hey, did you hear about that new mass spectrometer the department just got?

B: Yeah, I heard it's really accurate.

A: I know, it can measure the mass of particles down to the atomic level.

B: That's pretty impressive. Do you think it can measure the weight of my heart after a bad breakup?

A: Uh, I don't think that's scientifically possible.

场景5：化学实验室中

A: Can you help me measure the pH of this solution?

B: Sure, let me grab the pH meter.

A: (watching as student B struggles with the equipment) Do you need any help?

B: No, I think I just need to calibrate it first.

A: (hears a loud explosion from the other side of the lab) Um, maybe we should worry about that first.

B: (turns to look) Yeah, good point. pH can wait.

【Write & Read】根据以下场景描述，写一篇实验室报告的简短介绍。

场景描述：你在实验室进行了一次流体力学实验，使用了压力传感器和流量计，测量了液体在管道中的压力和流量。你需要写一份简短的实验报告，介绍实验的目的、使用的仪器和测量结果。

Experimental Report

The purpose of this experiment was to measure the pressure and flow rate of liquid in a pipeline using pressure sensors and flow meters.

The experiment was conducted in the laboratory of Fluid Mechanics. The experimental setup consisted of a pipeline with a pressure sensor and a flow meter installed at different points along the pipeline.

The pressure sensor was used to measure the pressure of the liquid in the pipeline, while the flow meter was used to measure the flow rate of the liquid.

The data obtained from the pressure sensor and flow meter were recorded and analyzed.

The results showed that the pressure and flow rate of the liquid varied at different points along the pipeline. These findings are important for understanding the behavior of fluids in pipelines and can be used to optimize industrial processes.

9

Chemical Production Practical English

搜一搜，
了解专业背景

化工生产过程有哪些
环节？

化工生产操作及控制
有哪些工作岗位？

搜一搜，
获取学习资源

化工生产过程的视频

化工生产过程的现场
图片

化工生产过程的英文
标识

化工生产过程常用术
语的中英文对照

9.1 Commonly Used English in Chemical Production

In chemical production sites, communication is crucial for ensuring safety, efficiency, and accuracy. Therefore, it is important to understand the commonly used English in chemical production sites.

(1) Control Room and Field Operations

In a chemical plant, the control room is the central location where operators can monitor and control various processes. The control room (Figure 9-1) is equipped with computer systems, alarms, and sensors that allow operators to observe and adjust the process parameters as needed. The field operations (Figure 9-2) are carried out in the plant's processing area, where equipment is installed to carry out the production process.

Figure 9-1   Polymer production control room

Figure 9-2　Styrene production field operation

(2) Special Operation Terminology

In chemical production, various special operations are carried out, such as handling of hazardous materials, waste disposal, and emergency response. It is important to use specific terminology to ensure clear communication among workers and to prevent accidents. Some examples of special operation terminology are listed below.

- Lockout/tagout: A safety procedure used to ensure that equipment is shut down and cannot be restarted until maintenance or repairs are complete.
- Confined space: An enclosed or partially enclosed area that is not designed for continuous human occupancy and has limited means of entry and exit.
- Hazardous waste: Waste that poses a substantial or potential threat to public health or the environment and requires special handling and disposal methods.

(3) Safety, Environmental Protection, Energy Conservation, and Emission Reduction Measures

Safety, environmental protection, energy conservation, and emission reduction are critical concerns in chemical production. The following measures can be taken to ensure safe and sustainable operations.

- Safety measures: Implement safety procedures, provide personal protective equipment, conduct safety training, and conduct regular safety audits.
- Environmental protection measures: Implement waste management procedures, monitor emissions, and reduce the use of hazardous materials.
- Energy conservation measures: Improve energy efficiency, reduce energy consumption, and utilize renewable energy sources.
- Emission reduction measures: Monitor and control emissions, improve process efficiency, and implement pollution control technologies.

（4）Public Utilities Facilities

Public utilities facilities are essential for supporting the operation of chemical plants.
- Water treatment plants: Treat and supply water to the chemical plant for use in various processes.
- Power plants: Generate electricity to power the chemical plant's equipment and processes.
- Waste treatment plants: Treat and dispose of waste generated by the chemical plant in an environmentally sound manner.

Conclusion

Effective communication, proper training, and the implementation of safety, environmental protection, energy conservation, and emission reduction measures are essential for safe and sustainable chemical production. The use of public utilities facilities, such as water treatment plants, power plants, and waste treatment plants, also plays a critical role in supporting chemical plant operations.

朗读二维码

专业词汇

- control room   控制室
- field operations   现场操作
- special operation   特种作业
- terminology   术语
- confined space   有限空间
- hazardous waste   危险废物
- emergency response   应急响应
- safety procedures   安全程序
- lockout/tagout   上锁 / 挂牌
- personal protective equipment (PPE)   个人防护装备
- environmental protection measures   环保措施

- waste management procedures　废物管理程序
- energy conservation measures　节能措施
- renewable energy sources　可再生能源
- emission reduction measures　减排措施
- pollution control technologies　污染控制技术
- water treatment plants　水处理厂
- power plants　电力厂

常用句型

- **Implement** safety procedures, **provide** personal protective equipment, **conduct** safety training, and **conduct** regular safety audits. 实施安全程序，提供个人防护设备，开展安全培训，并定期进行安全审计。

【句型解释】这是一个典型的并列祈使句结构，四个祈使句并列，前三个用逗号分隔，最后一个用连词"and"连接。并列结构可以使指令清晰有序，适合列举多项任务或步骤。连词"and"用于连接最后一项，表示列举的结束。

【例句】We need to implement safety procedures, **provide** personal protective equipment, and **conduct** safety training to ensure the safety of our workers.

我们需要实施安全程序，提供个人防护设备，并进行安全培训，以确保人员的安全。

互动练习

- What is the control room in a chemical plant? (　　)
   A) A room where waste is disposed of
   B) A room where operators can monitor and control various processes
   C) A room where employees take breaks
   D) A room where safety audits are conducted
- What is the purpose of lockout/tagout in chemical production? (　　)
   A) To ensure equipment is shut down and cannot be restarted until maintenance or repairs are complete
   B) To reduce energy consumption
   C) To treat and dispose of waste generated by the chemical plant
   D) To monitor and control emissions

- What are some measures that can be taken to ensure safe and sustainable chemical production? (   )
  A) Implement safety procedures, provide personal protective equipment, conduct safety training, and conduct regular safety audits
  B) Use hazardous materials and ignore environmental concerns
  C) Utilize non-renewable energy sources
  D) Disregard emission control technologies
- What is the purpose of public utilities facilities in chemical production? (   )
  A) To generate hazardous waste
  B) To treat and dispose of waste generated by the chemical plant
  C) To reduce energy consumption
  D) To support the operation of the chemical plant
- What are hazardous wastes in chemical production? (   )
  A) Waste that poses a substantial or potential threat to public health or the environment and requires special handling and disposal methods
  B) Waste that can be disposed of normally
  C) Waste that is recycled
  D) Waste that is used as raw material

9.2 Common Spoken English in Chemical Production

朗读二维码

　　Effective communication is crucial in the chemical industry to ensure safe and efficient production. Here are some common spoken English phrases and expressions used in chemical production.

(1) Safety Precautions

- "Remember to wear your personal protective equipment (PPE) at all times."
- "Make sure to properly label all hazardous materials."
- "Let's review the safety procedures before starting the job."
- "If there's an emergency, activate the alarm and evacuate the area immediately."
- "Never hesitate to report any safety concerns to your supervisor."

(2) Operating Equipment

- "We need to calibrate the instruments before starting the process."
- "Check the pressure gauge before opening the valve."
- "Start the pump slowly and monitor the flow rate."

- "Adjust the temperature to the desired set point."
- "Remember to flush the line with water after cleaning."

(3) Troubleshooting

- "What seems to be the problem? Let's troubleshoot together."
- "Did you check the power supply? That might be the issue."
- "Maybe we need to replace the faulty sensor."
- "Let's isolate the problem and find a solution."
- "If we can't fix it, we need to escalate the issue to the maintenance team."

(4) Work Instructions

- "Can you provide me with the Standard Operating Procedure (SOP)?"
- "Make sure to follow the batch record instructions step-by-step."
- "We need to perform a quality control check before releasing the product."
- "Remember to document all the process parameters and observations."
- "Let's do a final inspection before shipping the product."

(5) General Conversation

- "How was your weekend? Did you do anything interesting?"
- "Did you hear about the new project we're starting next month?"
- "I'm feeling a bit overwhelmed. Can you help me with this task?"
- "Thanks for your hard work. Let's finish this batch strong."
- "Don't forget to submit your time card before leaving today."

Conclusion

By familiarizing yourself with these common spoken English phrases and expressions, you can improve your communication skills and ensure a safe and efficient chemical production process.

专业词汇

- safety precautions 安全措施

朗读二维码

Part 3 Practical English for Chemical Engineering

- hazardous materials 危险物质
- emergency 紧急情况
- alarm 警报
- evacuate 撤离
- supervisor 主管
- operating equipment 操作设备
- calibrate 校准
- instruments 仪器

常用句型

- We **need to** calibrate the instruments before starting the process. 我们需要在开始流程之前校准仪器。

【句型解释】该句型包含了一个常见的科技英语表达：**need to** + verb 原形。在这个句子中，**need to** 表示必须要做的事情，calibrate 是动词原形，表示调校仪器。这种句型常用于科技工作场合中，强调必须按照规定的步骤去做某些事情。

【例句】We **need to** analyze the data before making a conclusion. 在得出结论之前，我们需要分析数据。

互动练习

- Which section of the text contains phrases related to safety in chemical production? (　　)
    A) Section (1)
    B) Section (2)
    C) Section (3)
    D) Section (4)
    E) Section (5)
- Which phrase suggests a solution-oriented approach to troubleshooting? (　　)
    A) "What seems to be the problem? Let's troubleshoot together."
    B) "Did you check the power supply? That might be the issue."
    C) "Maybe we need to replace the faulty sensor."
    D) "Let's isolate the problem and find a solution."
    E) "If we can't fix it, we need to escalate the issue to the maintenance team."

- What should you do before releasing a product according to the text? (   )

  A) Follow the batch record instructions step-by-step

  B) Calibrate the instruments

  C) Adjust the temperature to the desired set point

  D) Flush the line with water after cleaning

  E) Perform a quality control check

- Which phrase is an example of a polite request? (   )

  A) "Start the pump slowly and monitor the flow rate."

  B) "Remember to document all the process parameters and observations."

  C) "Can you provide me with the Standard Operating Procedure (SOP)?"

  D) "Let's review the safety procedures before starting the job."

  E) "Thanks for your hard work. Let's finish this batch strong."

- Which phrase indicates that the speaker is feeling overwhelmed? (   )

  A) "How was your weekend? Did you do anything interesting?"

  B) "Did you hear about the new project we're starting next month?"

  C) "I'm feeling a bit overwhelmed. Can you help me with this task?"

  D) "Thanks for your hard work. Let's finish this batch strong."

  E) "Don't forget to submit your time card before leaving today."

Exercises

【Speak & Listen】化工生产现场的对话

A: Hey, do you know what that machine does?

B: No, I don't. Let's go ask the operator.

A: Excuse me, sir. What does this machine do?

Operator: Well, this is a distillation column. It separates the different components of a mixture by their boiling points.

A: Wow, sounds like magic.

B: Yeah, like a giant witch's cauldron.

Operator: (laughs) Yeah, you could say that.

A: So, how does it work exactly?

Operator: Well, we heat up the mixture until it boils, and the vapor rises up the column. Then, as it cools down, the different components condense at different heights and we collect them separately.

B: Fascinating. It's like a tower of liquid Legos.

Operator: (laughs) I guess you could say that too.

A: Thanks for explaining it to us.

B: Yeah, now we can impress our friends with our newfound knowledge of distillation columns.

Operator: Anytime. Just don't forget to wear your safety gear and follow the protocols.

【Write & Read】假设你在一家化工企业实习,负责某一生产线的监控和维护。请根据以下情景,向主管报告生产线出现的问题。

情景:你注意到生产线中的一个温度传感器故障了,并且生产线的输出量下降了。你已经检查了所有的连接和电源,但是问题仍然存在。请向主管报告此事,并说明你的建议。

范文

To: Production Line Supervisor
Subject: Temperature Sensor
Malfunction and Decreased Output

Dear Supervisor,

I am writing to report a problem that I have noticed on the production line that I am responsible for monitoring and maintaining. One of the temperature sensors on the line has malfunctioned, and as a result, the output of the line has decreased.

I have thoroughly checked all the connections and power sources related to the sensor, but the problem still persists. I suggest that we replace the sensor as soon as possible to restore the normal production output.

Please let me know how we can proceed with replacing the sensor and any other actions that we need to take to prevent such issues in the future.

Thank you for your attention to this matter.
Sincerely,
[Your Name]

Reference

[1] 符德学. 化学化工专业英语. 3版. 北京：化学工业出版社，2011.

[2] 齐藤胜裕，增田秀树. 化学版 これを英語で言えますか. 东京：讲谈社，2012.

[3] 王俊文，张仲林. 化工基础与创新实验. 北京：国防工业出版社，2014.

[4] 冷士良，阮浩. 化工文献检索实用教程. 2版. 北京：化学工业出版社，2014.

[5] 梁凤凯，陈学梅. 有机化工生产技术与操作. 2版. 北京：化学工业出版社，2015.

[6] 程宝家，杜爱华，Martin v D，等. 阿朗新科合成橡胶手册. 北京：化学工业出版社，2022.

[7] 陈敏恒. 化工原理（少学时）. 3版. 上海：华东理工大学出版社，2019.

[8] 陈甘棠. 化学反应工程. 4版. 北京：化学工业出版社，2021.

[9] 陈炳和. 化学反应过程与设备. 4版. 北京：化学工业出版社，2020.

[10] Fogler H S. Elements of Chemical Reaction Engineering. 6th ed. London: Pearson, 2020.

[11] Levenspiel O. Chemical Reaction Engineering. 3rd ed. 北京：化学工业出版社，2002.

[12] 刘承先，文艺. 化学反应器操作实训. 北京：化学工业出版社，2006.

[13] Schwetlick K. 有机合成实验室手册. 22版. 北京：化学工业出版社，2012.

[14] 陈国桓，张喆，许莉，等. 化工机械基础. 4版. 北京：化学工业出版社，2021.

[15] 蒋作良. 药厂反应设备及车间工艺设计. 北京：中国医药科技出版社，2008.

[16] 袁渭康，王静康，费维扬，等. 化学工程手册. 3版. 北京：化学工业出版社，2019.

[17] Khodabakhshi E, Blom P W M, Michels J J. Efficiency enhancement of polyfluorene: Polystyrene blend light-emitting diodes by simultaneous trap dilution and β-phase formation. Applied Physics Letters, 2019, (114), 093301.